OLD COUNTRY STORES OF NEW HAMPSHIRE

BRUCE D. HEALD

Charleston   London

THE
History
PRESS

Old Country Stores *of* New Hampshire

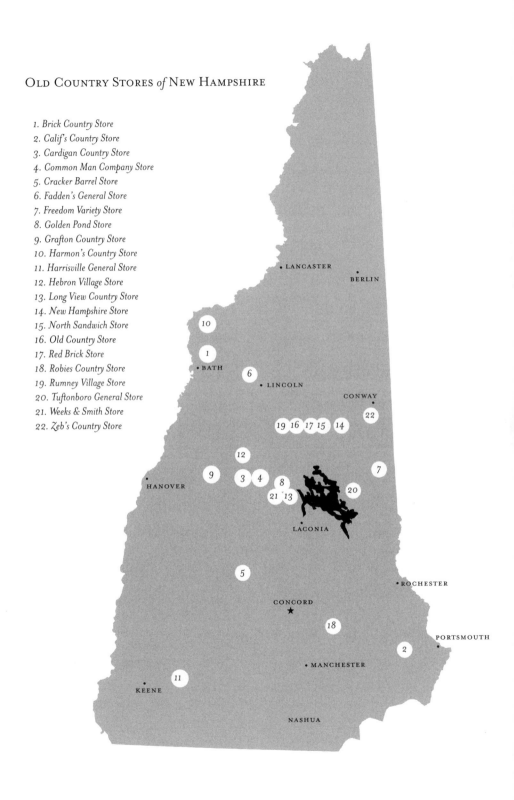

Published by The History Press
Charleston, SC 29403
www.historypress.net

Front cover, top left: Fadden's General Store, N. Woodstock. *Top right*: The Ashland Common Man Company Store, Ashland. *Bottom*: The Old Country Store, Moltonborough. *Back cover, left*: Fadden's General Store, N. Woodstock. *Right*: Zeb's Country Store, N. Conway.

First published 2013

Manufactured in the United States

ISBN 978.1.60949.981.5

Library of Congress CIP data applied for.

Contents

Acknowledgements

I would like to extend my appreciation to the following people and organizations that made this history possible: Maxine and Brenda Aldrich, John and Glenn Anzaldi, Vinny Bianco, Steve and Nancy Bleiler, Greg Bolton, Ray Boutin, Calaf's, Maryanne Canfield, Lois Carmody, David and Debra Chouinard, Kenneth Cushing, Jennie Eastman, Jim Fadden, Carol Foord, Nancy B. Foster, Freedom Historical Society, Roselyn Grossholz, Majorie Gene Harkness, Jim Harrison, Harrisville Historical Society, Greg and Teri Heppe, Deborah Herrington, Steve Holden, Edward S. Leonard, Nancy and Thomas Lindsey, Mike and Nancy Lusby, Paul and Marilyn McGuire, Meredith Historical Society, Steve Merrill, Moultonborough Public Library, Russell Partras, Lloyd and Dorothy Robie, Miranda Sandahl, Sandwich Historical Society, Michael Shattuck, Lois R. Shea, Pat and Bill Simon, Karen Tolman, Tuftonboro Public Library and Zeb's General Store.

Introduction

The romance and enchantment of a general store begin when you enter and sniff the deep aroma of many spices, tobacco and the stove with its burning fragrance so distinct it can dissolve the years off any aging country boy. Not just any store in the village could muster this fragrance simply because most everything sold in other stores is packaged.

The general store's bouquet came from its huge coffee mill, as bright red as a fire engine; its great tin canisters of bulk tea; and a vast cabinet of lesser canisters containing cinnamon bark, allspice, cloves and nutmeg seeds from which emanated the combined incense of India and the other spice countries. Now add to this a mild dose of kerosene tinged strongly with salt salmon and dried cod.

This was only the beginning, not the sum total, of the general store's fragrance. Modifying it were the milder and quite indescribable smells of unbleached muslin and the display of rubber and felt boots, buckle rubbers and moccasins. Combining with these was the pungency of pounds of plug tobacco, each cut marked with a tin tag denoting Spearhead and Everyday Smoke, and the small open barrel labeled Pittsburgh Stogies. These were the major balms and musky aromas that blended to produce the heavenly redolence of the general store.

There were no signs to designate the various departments. You had to look, and in looking you could find that there was, spread before your eyes, almost everything that man, woman or child could need. Hence, cant dogs stood in a corner next to the yard goods. Flyspecked straw hats and new woolen mittens were suspended on a wire above the shelves of patent medicines, whose labels testified to as powerful a belief in miracles as if the bottles had contained vitamins instead of painkillers and pectorals and invigorators.

What were truly important among the general store's departments were the village post office and the village forum in the shape and style of a box-stove, a couple of chairs and a box of sawdust.

It seemed customary that most of the men who socialized at the store performed one of three talents very well. They could whittle, chew tobacco and, of course, play checkers.

Jim Harrison reminisces these talents in his book *Country Stores* with the following memories:

> *Whittling was an aimless diversion that often served merely to prevent the knife handler from having to look up while discussing matters at hand. Using razor sharp Barlow's, most whittlers just made long, thin shavings that curled up around their brogan-clad feet.*
>
> *Some of the craftsmen would cut out crude forms and faces, only to smooth them out again, but most found satisfaction in making long, burnished surfaces.*

Chewing tobacco cultivated some crude habits in the store, thus signs were posted. Harrison reveals the following excerpts:

> *Signs saying, "If You Spit on Your Floor at Home, Go Home and Spit" and "Smokers and Chewers Please Spit on Each Other and Not the Stove" were prominently displayed, but never taken seriously by tobacco-chewing customers. Sandboxes near the stove and brass spittoons did their part but could not remove the temptation to spit elsewhere. A tolerant storeowner, who sold the tobacco in the first place, was obliged to maintain the arena for the mouth-muscled activities of the participants.*
>
> *The chance to hit the hot stove with a mouthful of tobacco juice and hear that "sizzling zing" was too tempting to pass up, especially for beginning chewers.*

Possibly the more popular moments of relaxation were spent in playing checkers and the related game, reverse checkers, usually known as "give away." Regular locals would gather in the store and play contentedly by the hour. Little conversation was exchanged, but all who were present enjoyed themselves, especially the players.

For the past fifty years, I have had a love affair with the old country store. A visit was a social event. We picked up the mail, groceries, a new pair of shoes and a pair of gloves. Don't forget the kitchen and farm tools. But times have changed, and the American spirit has changed. Convenience stores and supermarkets are replacing the village store. There appears to be a disregard for quality, and disposable items and quick-wrap foods are its replacements. Today, methods of purchasing stock have greatly changed as well. Gone are the old-time peddlers and traveling salesmen who spent days on the road and slept at local inns.

Now many of the old buildings—stores, barns, linen and textile mills—are either abandoned or torn down to be replaced with a mall, office building or parking lot. There goes the old railroad depot, which was the envy of the small-town landscape.

Country Stores also addresses the ageless treatise on the old buildings:

Before pulling down a building in pleasing decay, it should be looked at three times…to be sure first, that it has no virtues in itself that will be sadly missed. Second, that it will not be missed as an enchantment of its present surroundings; third that it might not form a useful point of focus, whether by agreement or by way of contrast in future surroundings.

Nevertheless, most of the present owners of country stores are proud to be the keepers of the keys to these pieces of local and state history. Here in this one, barn-like room was concentrated the life of the town as it touched matters federal, social, medical, civic and mercantile.

This historic emporium, which we call the country store, is intended to celebrate the lasting heritage and nostalgia of the Granite State. Within the contents of this book are found historic glimpses of some of the oldest and most unique country stores in the state of New Hampshire, and I will endeavor to expound on the true essence of the days past that is being kept alive today in the state. Unfortunately, not all the stores were included, but we should be assured those not mentioned are equally important to our New Hampshire heritage. We should never let the old country store be forgotten.

Chapter 1

Origin of the Old Country Store

The forerunners of the store merchants during the early settlement of New Hampshire were the peddlers with their carts full of merchandise. These were the days of the horse and buggy. They traveled by foot and wagon and carried a backpack or trunk. Some peddlers rode horseback with saddlebags that were filled with merchandise. Such items may have included necessities for the home and farm such as spoons, needles and pins, knives, spices of all kinds and other small objects that were easy to carry from town to town. It was not uncustomary to barter, for there was little currency available and no banks nearby.

Most of the farmers and their families made everything necessary for survival. Farmers seldom lived close to one another, thus they had to travel several miles to do their trading with their neighbors.

As time passed and settlements were established, a local trading post became the meeting place where they traded and swapped their products for those of other farmers. The trading post became a country (or general) store, which serviced the settlers. It connected the farms into one community.

The store was the meeting place for town affairs and was always filled with the local citizens of the community. The politician, the barber, the postman, the carpenter and the millers all seemed to be making deals with their neighbors. You might have found them sitting around the stove or on a bench located on the front porch. Inside the store, you might have seen the villagers playing cards, checkers or just plain arguing about local politics. The assemblage of loungers who graced the front stoop of the general store in the summer and arranged themselves around the stove in

The peddlers in horses and buggies were possibly the first traveling merchants to sell household and farm supplies in New Hampshire. *Courtesy of author's collection.*

the winter usually drifted in during the morning to get their mail and read the announcements that had been tacked up since the day before: "There would be the Methodist church supper this Saturday night. A box social was to be held at the Grange Hall, and Millie Abbott needed help for the Quimby School booth at the Sandwich Fair."

Those settlers who were not farmers would set up shops in the village, with the general store as the magnet. Sometimes the regulars would make a small purchase and then sit until somebody said it was time to go home. Here was the pulse of the community where the village came alive and people had contact with the outside world.

There is a common anecdote of one man who waited all morning for the mail, and when it came, he started waiting for the afternoon mail: "Gosh, half-past ten, and I promised my wife I'd be home by ten." Then he settled back with the remark, "Well, she's mad as she can be now. Might's well stay another hour."

You would generally recognize the store by its exterior shape. It was usually a two-story building, centrally located in the village. The front of the store often had two large display windows on either side of the door.

One window would display items of interest for the ladies—hats, clothing material, buttons and dolls—while the other window would have articles such as tools and shoes for the men.

Most country stores had platforms or wooden sidewalks built in front of them. The front porch was a familiar feature of the store and was well worn by years of sitting, smoking and spitting. More than likely, no two boards of the porch would be level, and the posts that supported the roof were likely to tilt in different directions. Many of these porches were built several feet above the ground, high enough to act as loading docks for deliveries to the store.

Because roads were not paved, the platform cut down on the amount of dirt that was brought into the store. When the farmers drove their wagons to the store, it was easier for them to load and unload onto the platform. There were usually two stone or iron posts on either side of the platform called "hitching posts" where horses and wagons were tied.

A sense of pride abided in the hearts and memories of the country people, and the storekeepers were no exception. The outer appearance of the building had to be inviting, for it was a matter of dignity to maintain the proper impression. Sometimes the façade would extend upward and hit the shingled, gable roof. The image of a tall storefront gave the look of a spacious interior. Wood-frame clapboards on the exterior permitted easy expansion as business grew and new construction was necessary. An additional outer building for extra stock and large equipment was sometimes needed for the store.

In the interior of many of the old country stores, we would find a conglomeration of merchandise. The store was a busy place at times when the necessities of life were made available, both by barter and sale.

The store would consist of a large room with small sections for dry goods, clothing, flour, kitchen gadgets, farm ware and other items, as well as a counter and large display cases that lined the side of the room. Cases and tables often formed an island in the center of the room, and wall space was covered with shelves and cabinets.

Most every country store had its own post office, and some still do. The only means of communication in the early days was the mail. Daily, the townspeople would come to the store's post office to pick up their mail. Each family had a separate cubbyhole in which the storekeeper placed the incoming mail. The mail was delivered by coach, and when it arrived, the storekeeper would sort the mail and send the outgoing mail with the coach. At the time, it could take up to two weeks to deliver the mail. Store owners were held to the same standards and duties as postmasters as historian Gerald Carson describes in the following observation:

A storekeeper who had gone before a magistrate and solemnly swore that he would support the Constitution of the United States, faithfully perform his duties as postmaster, and abstain from everything forbidden by the laws in relation to post offices and post roads within the United States; a man in whose Ability, Integrity, and Prudence the President of the United States had reposed special confidence—a man once accustomed to such responsibilities and honors, could not look on unmoved when he saw a diminishment in his stamp sales and the dignity of his position.

Telephones didn't appear until the 1880s, but even then they were too expensive for the common home; so often the nearest phone was located in the country store. Most storekeepers let their customers use the phone at no cost; however, some charged a fee for its use.

Needless to say, everyone knew everyone else's business, for local news spread quickly via the country store. Customers looked forward to hearing the latest gossip while doing the shopping. While the chatting was going on, they could read the latest announcements concerning community affairs and town meetings on the outside wall of the store by the porch.

The village store became the hub of business and the center of activities, essentially the center of the village. These small towns would have had other stores, such as a barbershop, a blacksmith shop, a cabinetmaker and stable tailors, as well as a community church and a one-room schoolhouse.

Town meetings were often held at the country store during the early days. Farmers would meet there to discuss their crops, and women would plan community social events. However, if there were a school or church in the village, the general store would only be used to transact business.

On Friday evening, the second floor of the store would be bustling with the activity of weekly dances. Families from far distances would gather at the social event and enjoy the music and square dancing.

Children would play on the front porch of the store while men sat around the stove and smoked their pipes or chewed tobacco. The men would bite a small piece of tobacco off a "plug," which was a big piece. As they chewed the tobacco, a dark liquid formed in their mouths that they would spit into a basket called a "spittoon" or, even better, a "cuspidor." If they missed their aim, the storekeeper's children had to clean the floor.

The proprietor of the Tuftonboro General Store is seen greeting you as you enter the store, 1902. *Courtesy of Greg and Teri Heppe.*

As you may have gathered, hospitality is the feeling experienced when entering the front door of the store. For those who recall experiences with such stores in New Hampshire, nostalgia imbues the atmosphere of the country stores still in existence today.

In the scene of a typical country store, one or two customers would be standing by the counter, in no hurry to run off. The proprietor would speak to the first customer in a low, easy tone before gradually filling his order by writing down figures on a brown paper package, leisurely adding them up (yawning comfortably) and accepting payment. Then the customer would unobtrusively leave, and the second would be likewise attended to.

Now it is your turn. Perhaps all you wanted was crackers and cheese. Quietly, the proprietor slices off the cheese with a large knife, and as you eat, you engage him in some political conversation of the day. Not heavy, intellectual repartee, just a slow chat, punctuated by many long pauses. The old clock ticks softly on the wall as a cat naps in the window among the dried fruit. Outside, the Concord Coach arrives to discharge a few passengers.

Axe helves, lumberman's stockings and felt boots, candy kisses and cans of beans wait patiently about. A wood chunk in the stove rolls over, and the proprietor puts in another log. The fire sings cheerily in the flue. Outside, you see it has begun to flurry.

A gust of wind throws snow against the doors with a raking noise. You hear the pawing of a horse and the creak of leather as the horse nudges at the hitching rack. Soon an old gentleman comes in. "It's snowing," he mutters.

He purchases some smoking tobacco, leisurely fills and lights his pipe and stands quietly gazing up and down the street. No one says anything. The clock goes on ticking; the store goes on living. It will be there tomorrow.

This was the place and these were the characters of local history. Here, as anthropologist might say, was the masculine in-group that handed down the oral tradition of colorful outlaws, departed captains and memories of lost causes.

Our New Hampshire story of the old village store would not be complete without including the various functions of these venerable crossroad emporiums.

Chapter 2

Stock and Trade

OLD COUNTRY STORE INVENTORY

The best way to describe the inside of the country store might be cluttered. Everything the storekeeper had to sell was put on display. In the main room of the store was usually a large wood-burning stove. The stove heated the store and also provided a cozy spot for conversation and playing checkers.

During the nineteenth and twentieth centuries, a customer who came into the country store didn't have a choice of brands. He or she simply asked for a slice of bacon, a wedge of cheese or a bag of flour. The clerk weighed out and wrapped each item and placed a price on the bag.

Generally speaking, the store was well stocked with dry goods, housewares, hardware, cloth, notions, seeds, books, medicine, tobacco, canned fruit, toys, candy and endless general merchandise.

NOT YOUR AVERAGE STORE

The real old country store is not your average store, for it is still set up as it might have looked before the turn of the century, often with five departments: dry goods, hardware, groceries, tobacco and butcher shop.

From the middle of the 1800s to the early 1900s, historian Roselyn Grossholz advises, the country store would have contained much of the following stock materials:

1. *A coffee mill (grinder), store sized with two wheels, hand operated, and in working condition.*
2. *A thread or spool cabinet of solid wood, usually walnut or oak, obtainable in a variety of styles and designs.*
3. *A wooden dye cabinet with colorful tin inserts and available in several sizes.*
4. *A hanging lamp, usually with an embossed metal font, tin or milk glass shade.*
5. *A scale, with platform and brass pan.*
6. *Display case, counter-top or floor standing.*
7. *A brass or iron cash register.*
8. *A store counter from 8 to 20 feet in length, with one drawer, usually of solid oak construction.*
9. *A floor caddy, 25 to 30 inches high or a wooden bin of the same size with original stenciling.*
10. *A shelf caddy, tin from 12 to 20 inches high.*
11. *An iron stove.*
12. *A wooden wall telephone.*

Materials from the early 1900s would contain at least the following items:

1. *An electric coffee grinder.*
2. *A thread cabinet of veneered wood or wood grained tin.*
3. *A tin dye cabinet.*
4. *Lighting fixture of the period.*
5. *Scale.*
6. *Display case.*
7. *Brass or wooden cash register.*
8. *Store counter.*
9. *Large shelf caddy with brand name.*
10. *Collection of at least a dozen individual tin containers varying from 1 to 10 pound size, with company names.*
11. *A stove, if required, or an advertising clock could be substituted.*
12. *A wall telephone or "candle-stick" style telephone.*

Today, many country stores in New Hampshire have expanded by adding the following items:

1. *One or more counters.*
2. *A merchandiser or grain counter. This has become a popular addition to the country store because many compartments are useful for displaying and dispensing.*
3. *A wooden chopping block.*
4. *A roll-top desk and swivel chair.*
5. *A set of shelf caddies from seven to twenty-two inches high with stenciled names of contents.*
6. *A barrel.*
7. *Store-size glass candy, peanut and gum jars.*
8. *A coffee roaster of the period.*
9. *Colorful advertising such as signs, posters, calendars, fans, trade cards, labels and thermometers.*
10. *Packing boxes and drums with colorful labels and imprinting.*
11. *A store counter stool.*
12. *A paper holder and cutter.*
13. *A string holder.*
14. *Store scoops of various sizes.*
15. *Fruit and vegetable bins.*
16. *An account file.*
17. *Additional scales in various designs and sizes.*
18. *Store "grabber" for reaching merchandise on shelves.*
19. *Additional counter display cases framed in wood, and metal, display stand of tin, and glass.*
20. *Additional floor standing display cases of wood and metal.*
21. *Post office unit.*
22. *An advertising regulator clock.*
23. *One or more additional cabinets with advertising, which contained veterinary and patent medicines, ink, dye, thread, sewing machine needles, hairnets, cosmetics, ribbons, hardware, spices, etc.*

The store merchant received most of his supplies in bulk, such as barrels of flour, crates of fruit, bags of cereal, dried beans and sugar and boxes of crackers. Coffee was usually green and had to be roasted at the store or at home, along with pepper, cloves and nutmeg. Tea was sold loose from a canister. Peas, beans, grains and rice were taken from drawers rather than canisters.

Once the order was complete, each item was measured, weighed, wrapped, tied and priced by the clerk. When paper bags came into use,

Interior of country store during the early 1900s. *Courtesy of Elmer L. Smith.*

the clerk would do the math of sales in pencil on the bag(s). In order to meet the competition from the larger grocery stores, weekly specials were promoted by distributing handbills.

It is true that the general store stocked tobacco products in many forms, including snuff and plug tobacco. It is interesting to note that there was a multitude of tobacco brands for sale, such as chewing, smoking, cigar and cigarette brands.

The wooden Indian, which may be seen in several New Hampshire general stores, was usually associated with tobacco and later became the emblem of the tobacco specialty shops. These carved wooden figures are now considered rare American folk art, and they were quite common as far back as the Civil War. Good examples of the Indian figure may be found on the front porch of the Old Country Store in Moultonborough and inside the Tuftonboro General Store. (Refer to chapter six for further information on the store Indian.)

Chewing tobacco was very popular and was available in either natural or flavored, such as the popular licorice. The early cigars of the nineteenth century were very popular to the country farmers in New Hampshire. The most expensive cigar was the Havana, then the domestic cigars followed by the least expensive, the stogie. The stogie was domestic tobacco that was a foot long. Most of the better tobacco was well packaged in colorful boxes and embossed with trademarks, which are collectable today.

Cigarettes were not as popular during the late nineteenth and early twentieth centuries, and by the time cigarettes dominated the tobacco counters, the general stores had passed their heyday in the retail market due to the larger chain stores.

For the collector, tobacco containers and advertisements are currently popular. A good way to display the tobacco items was with large advertising signs and posters that could line the wall. Other inducements for promotional advertisements were counter displays and wall lighters. Storekeepers went so far as rewarding the customers with picture cards and premiums for prizes. Other suggestions for continuing this tobacco theme are spelled out by Grossholz:

1. *Barrels and drums of bulk tobacco with interesting tax stamps from the late 1800s, as well as printing and levels.*
2. *Wooden cigar boxes, may feature colorful pictures, which may resemble early valentines, or have pictures of the founder of the company, or carry such names as The Judge, Two Orphans, Minty's Own, Virginny Cheroots, etc.*
3. *Counter-top cigar humidor-dispensers of tin and glass with inserts of pictures and advertising.*
4. *Iron cut-plug cutters, counter-top and wall-mounted models.*

5. *Iron cigarette dispensing machines.*

6. *Tin or iron penny match-dispensers.*

7. *Cigar lighter/cutters, alcohol or gas operated, made of combinations of iron, brass, and tin, usually with embossed advertising and/or pictures in glass inserts. They were usually sold to a store after it was proved that the volume of business of a certain brand or cigar warranted such installation.*

8. *Tobacco advertising posters and signs in porcelain, tin, cardboard and paper, pertaining to scrap, cut-plug, cigars, cigarettes, snuff and pipe tobacco.*

9. *The owner of a genuine antique hand-carved full size American Indian will add greatly to the display.*

10. *A tobacco advertising thermometer, and old calendars with tobacco advertisements.*

During the 1800s, the country stores supplied the ladies' department with fabrics, trimmings and sewing notions. Often, linen and wool fabrics were woven at home.

A clothing display during the 1800s included a full array of notions, trimming and other decorative materials, namely ribbons, shoes, gloves, bonnets, bolts of fabrics and other accessories of the time.

Men's clothing was also displayed in the French fashion magazines. Many gentlemen preferred the illustrations found in such magazines as *Puck*, published in New York. Several copies of this publication during the late 1890s demonstrated that the styles had not changed for at least fifty years. Coats were long and straight. Trousers were designed with a front panel, which buttoned on the side. The shirts had stiff, detachable collars, which were worn with bow and string ties. Derbies or top hats and spats completed the outfit.

Grossholz continues with other ways for displaying clothing goods:

1. *Hat and wig stand of cast iron.*

2. *Wooden glove forms.*

3. *Dress forms with decorative cast iron of tin standards.*

4. *Manikins or cloth-covered figure forms.*

5. *Small display cases.*

6. *Advertising material in the form of signs and fans, calendars, and catalogs.*

7. *Wood and glass ribbon cases with drop or sliding doors.*

8. *Mirrors mounted or hand mirrors.*

9. *Bolt and rolls of dress and suit material.*

Candy counter with Katarina Prieberova posing in front at Zeb's Country Store in North Conway, New Hampshire. *Courtesy of David Peterson and Zeb's Country Store.*

Farm supplies were a staple and well stocked, seeds being a popular item. By the 1860s, garden seeds were colorfully packaged in the hopes that it would stimulate the sales of the seed products. One popular producer and distributor was Charles W. Briggs from Rochester, New York. In partnership with his brother, they became known as the Briggs Brothers. The company's display packaging of the seeds gained the attention of the country stores and became a very popular item.

Finally, parents beware—the candy counter is located right up front in most country or general stores. As adults, we remember being drawn to the jawbreakers, all-day suckers and candy canes. Kids have not changed.

The variety available was endless, and the selection was almost enchanting to the young buyer. In order to make up one's mind, a thorough inventory through the glass case had to be taken and then the difficult process of selecting the right candies undertaken. The process of shopping was unhurried and included the anticipation of the pleasure of the purchase.

Now came the time to purchase the items. It was fascinating to watch the storekeeper measure each of the selections of candy. An imaginative candy producer would constantly present new items, including orange sugar peanuts, Mary Janes, Tootsie and jawbreakers.

Do you remember when the only way to say, "I love you" was with a bag of candy from the country store?

Indeed, I remember the penny candy counter at the old store and how we looked forward to shopping there. In those early days, you could buy five jaw busters for a penny, as well as many other brightly colored candies for the same price. Sometimes, when the storekeeper noticed a young customer with no money look toward the candy counter, he would take sympathy on the youngster and generously give him a piece free of charge. There was a time in the early days of the general store when the proprietor would take pride in the amount of candy he gave away free of charge.

The most popular pieces of candy were the peppermint sticks. It must have been the red and white stripe that attracted the eyes. Another favorite was the all-day suckers. The memories of the candy counter at the country store are of its being colorful and well stocked. And so it still is displayed today, just to test the customer's endurance.

Chapter 3

Home Remedies

Contrary to the name's indication, patent medicines were not patented in the way we think of the term today. The remedies were considered secret formulas of the inventor or owner, who used the term "patent" (which might suggest the medicine formula's submission to the U.S. government's Patent Office) to mean uniqueness in the qualities of the formula or some new use for its application. On the other hand, if a U.S. patent had been granted, the remedy would not have been considered a secret. According to the U.S. Patent Office, "its composition would have to appear in the patent specifications." This was the last thing a doctor or storekeeper would desire. It implied that the names were simply trade names that had been registered by the U.S. government as a name of that particular property.

The owners of a particular medicine or medical business could have been self-proclaimed doctors, Indians, pharmacists, professors or corporations who personalized their products very carefully when dealing with the public.

On the label, a brand name or image would be applied, such as a doctor who may appear in a white coat, signifying him as a man of science. He may be illustrated in an advertisement with a test tube, announcing a special discovery about vitamins—a cure-all remedy.

It is interesting to note that the only products that had brand names were tonics and medicines. The tonics would promise to cure almost every ailment from corns to stomach pains. In fact, most of the tonics were made of the same ingredients, namely quinine and alcohol. The most popular brands were "Dr. Jones' Fabulous Cure-all" and "Dr. Haley's Elixir and Tonic." In New Hampshire, there was one nameless storekeeper who favored "Warner's

Safe Nervine." This medicine was fine for cuts, sick dogs and soothing the stomach. The medicine, which was taken by mouth, was also used as an ointment for cuts and sores. If the remedies were not located in the store, the apothecary shop sometimes was located near the rear of the store. The apothecary was the town pharmacist or druggist and was often the doctor as well.

Possibly the best advice was to "feed a cold, starve a fever." It has been my experience that no doctor or storekeeper entirely dismisses the possibilities of mind over matter.

Cure-all medicines, which remain on the market today, were some of the most trusted mixtures that came out of the disreputable industry. Father John's Cough Syrup, Sloan's Chill Tonic, Black Draught and Lydia Pinkham seemed to have weathered both the test of time and the eyes of the federal regulatory agencies.

The traveling doctors dispensed their medicines to patients and sold them to general stores at wholesale prices. The general stores did quite well with the patent medicine sales. Besides the medicine, the doctor had small instruments with which he made tiny holes in the patient's flesh in order to allow the "bad blood" to flow out. When the patient had an infection that could not be healed on an arm or leg, doctors cut the arm or leg off. No matter what the remedy was, it was usually painful. There were no anesthetics in those days.

Many times, doctors had no understanding of an illness and could not adequately treat the patient who suffered from unfamiliar ailments. These ailments may have come from emotional disorders, such as depressed or catatonic moods, and periods of hallucination, which were usually classified as "the devil's making."

SUGGESTED HOME REMEDIES

When the doctors were not available, the country storekeepers often advised the customer of some remedies that he might have in the store or just the use of common sense. Our forefathers in New Hampshire were always conscious of the betterment of their health and well-being, and so they, with the aid of the storekeeper, set guidelines and suggestions for the cures of the most common of ills.

Almanacs, medical journals and home doctoring books promoted simple remedy relief during the nineteenth century. The earliest country stores

Hite's Pain Cure
Contains
ALCOHOL 65%
Oils, Gums, &tc.
Guaranteed under the FOOD and
DRUGS ACT, June 10, 1906. N. 2184

The lettering above is from a stencil used by Hite's for shipping cartons and crates. The company later moved to Roanoke, Virginia.

The pain cure contained 65% alcohol. Its main contribution was that it came in very small bottles!

The Barker's Almanac was given away to country stores with the wholesale purchase of the products. The store in turn sold it or gave it away at the operator's discretion. Book marks were given with the purchase of Mennen's powders and cosmetics.

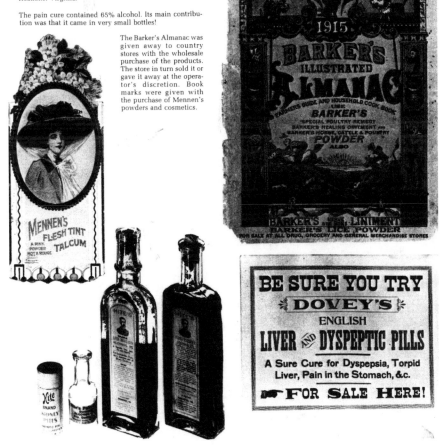

This would be a typical advertisement of the home remedies displayed in the country store, late 1800s. *Courtesy of Elmer L. Smith.*

carried books on home medicine, and their shelves were filled with remedy supplies to supplement nature's agents. Kerosene, turpentine, castor oil, baking soda and catgut were available items that supplemented the natural herb roots, leaves and animal fats that were maintained as the basics in any home medicine cabinet.

A fine example of this cure-all remedy method is given by Gerald Carson in *The Old Country Store*:

> *Dr. J.C. Ayer's Sarsaparilla was recommended for a harrowing list of disorders, including a very deep-seated one, "debility peculiar to spring." It contained "the Sarsaparilla-root of the tropics, Stillingia, Yellow Dock, Mandrake, and other roots held in high repute." No quantitative detail, of course; and no mention of spiritus frumenti, which was what did the business.*
>
> *The folkways of nineteenth-century America seem perplexing and inconsistent to us today. It was a time of prudery and sticky sentiment, mixed with a coarse realism worthy of a Restoration wit. A leg was a limb, or did not exist at all. Yet, widely circulated patent medicine advertisements dealt with a frightening list of symptoms; nor were they dainty when it came to a discussion of piles or tubercles.*
>
> *The wounds, diseases, and impaired health of a soldier who returned from the Civil War introduced the mental patterns of ill-health and self-medication. The printed word, in its abundance, spread news to the remotest villages of cured and recoveries no less startling than the miracles performed in ancient days.*

Patent medicine was a popular item and well displayed in the country store. According to Elmer L. Smith's *The Country Store*, newspaper advertising played a large role in bringing medicine to the stores:

> *The hard work led to plenty of aches and pains—thus a demand for convenient ready-made remedies for common ailments. This demand was met by more than 3,000 medicine makers, marketing more than 10,000 brand names and labels. Sales reached around 300,000,000 bottles or containers a year. It was a big business. Ready made (so-called Patent) Medicines became available in most country stores through demand created by local newspaper advertisements. It has been estimated that 20,000 local papers ran patent medicine ads at the turn of the century. It is noted that Lydia E. Pinkham's Vegetable Compound was promoted with $50,000.00*

in newspaper and magazine advertising! Little wonder the local crossroads store stocked shelves of various medicines.

The country store proprietor may suggest that customers consider sarsaparilla, sassafras, rabbit tobacco and various tree barks that had value as curative agents and remind them not to forget mother's brewed healing herbal tea for ailing youngsters. The following folk medicine from the North Country is hereby passed to us; they lived by it faithfully for their total existence and survival:

In consideration of their sleeping habits, it was advised by our local doctor, or storekeeper, that it was better to go to sleep on the right side; for then the stomach was in the position of a bottle turned upside-down, and the contents of it were aided in passing out by gravitation. It was also suggested that if one goes to sleep on the left side, the operation of emptying the stomach of its contents was more like drawing water from the well. After going to sleep, let the body take its own position. If you sleep on your back, especially after a hearty meal, the weight of the digestive organs, and that of the food resting on the great vein of the body near the backbone, compressing it, and arrests the flow of the blood more or less. If the arrest is partial, the sleep is disturbed and there will be unpleasant dreams.

For persons who eat three times a day, it is amply sufficient to make the last meal of cold bread and butter and a cup of warm drink. No one can starve on it; while the perseverance in the habit soon begets a vigorous appetite for breakfast, so promising of a day of comfort. Our village physician makes the following suggestion for the sickroom:

In preparing a meal for anyone whose appetite is delicate, it should be made to look as tempting as possible. The tray should be covered with the whitest napkin, and the silver, glass and china should shine with cleanliness. There should not be too great a variety of viands, but a very small portion of each one. Nothing more quickly disgusts a feeble appetite than a quantity of food presented at one time. The patient should never be consulted beforehand as to what he or she will eat or drink. If they ask for anything, give it to them, with the doctor's permission; otherwise prepare something that they are known to like, and offer it without previous comment.

In the question of hot weather and sunstroke, it is common knowledge that the following suggestions be followed:

Sunstroke is caused by excessive heat, and especially if the weather is muggy. It is more apt to occur on the second, third or fourth day of a heat spell than on the first. Loss of sleep, worry, excitement, close sleeping room, deliberate use of stimulants predisposed to it. It is more apt to attack those working in the sun, and especially between the hours of eleven in the morning and four in the afternoon. If working in the sun, wear a light hat, not black as it absorbs the heat, straw, etc., and put inside of it a wet clothe or a large green leaf. Do not check perspiration, but drink what water you need to keep it up. Perspiration prevents the body from being overheated. If a feeling of dizziness, headache or exhaustion occurs, cease work immediately, lie down in a shady and cool place; apply cold cloth and pour cold water over the head and neck.

If anyone is overcome by heat, send immediately for the nearest good physician. While waiting for the physician, give the person cold drinks of water, cold black tea or cold coffee, if able to swallow. If the skin is hot, sponge with or pour cold water over the body or limbs, and apply to the head pounded ice wrapped in a towel or other cloth. If there is no ice available, keep a cold cloth on the head and pour cold water on it as well as the body. If the person is pale, very faint and pulse feeble, let him inhale ammonia in two tablespoonfuls of water with a little sugar. (1880 New York Board of Health.)

An unknown historian recorded that the storekeeper would probably give the customer this folk medicine advice:

The less a man drinks in hot weather the better, for the more we drink the more we want to drink, until even ice water palls and becomes of metallic taste. Hence the longer you can put off drinking cold water on the morning of a hot day, the better you will feel at night. Drinking largely at meals, even cold water, or simple tea, is a mere habit and is always hurtful. No one should drink at any one meal more than a quarter of a pint of any liquid, even cold water, for it always retards, impairs and interferes with the healthful digestion.

If you sleep at all in the daytime it will interfere with the soundness of your sleep at night much less if the nap be taken in the afternoon.

A short nap in the daytime may be necessary to some. Let it not exceed ten minutes. To this end, sleep with the forehead resting on a chair-back or edge of a table. Now, let us consider the common cold. It is recommended that you first take a large teaspoonful of flax-seed, with two pennyworth of licorice and a quarter of pound of raisins. Put it into two quarts of soft water, and let simmer over a slow fire till it reduces to one. Then add it to a pound of brown sugar candy, pounded, and a tablespoonful of white wine vinegar or lemon juice. It is best to drink the vinegar as you take it, and then drink half a pint on going to bed, and take a little when the cough is troublesome. It generally cures within two or three days, and some that have almost settled in two or three weeks.

It is common knowledge that when anyone has sleigh sickness, a piece of fish-skin applied to the pit of the stomach—this would be a capital cure. A good cure for inflamed eyes would be to pour boiling water on elderflowers and steep them like tea. When cold, put three or four drops of laudanum into a small glass of elder tea, and let some of the mixture run into the eyes, three or four times a day. The eyes will become perfectly strong in the course of a week, I think.

For stings of insects, moisten common whiting or chalk pounded very fine with cold water and apply it immediately for a few minutes; neither pain nor swelling will ensue.

In the case of a bad appetite—First clean the stomach with a dose of physic. Then prepare a 1–2 oz. Quassia, 1–2 gentian, by steeping till the strength is out in one pint of water, strain and add a pint of brandy, with sugar: Half a wine glass before breakfast and dinner.

For indigestion—Keep the bowels open with castor oil or rhubarb. If it attends with severe pain, apply a strong mustard poultice. Piles may be cured by keeping the bowels open and anoint the external parts with cod liver oil. This is a new but excellent remedy.

For heartburn—Eat a small piece of raw carrot; it will give a certain relief. Don't laugh—just try it.

For wind—Drink hot tea or peppermint water, 20 drops of vitriol in a glass of water, twice a day will give permanent relief.

Diarrhea—Live a few days on a light dry diet with moderate exercise. Take pepper tea and use a little rhubarb as a medicine.

Toothache—Use a wet piece of cotton with the oil of tar and clove. It will give almost immediate relief.

If the one has a fever, first cleanse the stomach and bowels, and afterwards keep up a moderate perspiration all over the body by drinking herb tea.

Many of these so-called remedies and wonder cures were believed to have come from the devil. Folk medicines were accepted by some and scorned by others, yet they kept alive some myths, such as these given by Carson:

Snake oil cures rheumatism.
Wash freckles away on the first day of May, with the morning dew.
For a cold, grease red flannel and wear it on the chest.
Put mud on a bee sting, or try a liniment made of St. John's wort
    and vinegar.
If the throat is sore, tie a piece of pork rind around the neck.
Sassafras tea clears the blood.
For heartburn, wear a match over the right ear.
If you step on a rusty nail, grease it and carry it in your pocket to
    prevent lockjaw.
Bury an old dishrag to drive away a wart.

Common home remedies coexist today with professional medical treatments, thus the old-fashioned folk cures have worked for many years; surely they must be given some medical credibility.

It was during the final years of the nineteenth century and the early years of the twentieth century that the drugstore, the traveling showman-doctor—with his Indian costume and minstrel shows—and the mail-order catalogues competed with the general country store for the patent medicine dollar. In 1905, a mail-order catalogue devoted several pages to their remedies.

Carson made the following observation:

> *It was enough to make a country merchant fighting mad to think of the money going through the post office window right under his nose. It was not only medicine, but everything else that people ought to buy at the home store—dress goods, button shoes, candy by the pail, all the thousands-odd articles to be found in a well run general merchandise store.*

Chapter 4

The Yankee Storekeeper

In this chapter, I have taken the liberty to embellish excerpts of a story by R.E. Gould, *Yankee Storekeeper*. Acting as the narrator, the Yankee Storekeeper relates to the reader what happens to the new owner of an early country store, his business and the goings-on of the store and his customers.

A gentleman and his family were looking to buy a country store, but their main concern was location. For all the surrounding communities to trade at their store, it would need to be located at the junction of a very large territory. Finally, the gentleman found the place that met his criteria. The narrative begins with the previous owner.

THE PURCHASE

The store had the usual stock: dry goods, hardware, farmer needs, groceries and kitchen utensils—a very fine start. Some extras that accompanied the store were bats, fly paper hanging over the groceries, cracker and pickle barrels, a pair of nose baskets and a clutter of books and children's games. This seemed to have been the predecessor's method of merchandising. The new proprietor bought the stock as is and felt like he had paid too much—a poor investment at $1,500 for the entire inventory.

His work was cut out for him.

One of his first concerns was to wash the floor, glass, shelves and display cabinets so the merchandise would have eye appeal. Shortly after, a drummer appeared at the front door. He seemed to have the answer by offering the following advice: "Hang four doors to cover those shelves and use that show case, and I'll put you in stock of $500 worth of hardware, and if it doesn't turn in sixty days, I'll take it back."

Beginning a new career was made with mixed feeling, and the taxes from the former owner had to be paid—he was damn mad.

He paid for the stock and $1,000 on the real estate. The previous owner was to take a mortgage for the balance. By the end of summer, he told the new proprietor that he was ready to make the deed but insisted on dating it back to April.

TIME FOR BUSINESS

Time passed, and he slowly became acquainted with the new business opportunities in his first New Hampshire town. The Yankee Storekeeper was a flatlander who had moved into a town full of natives—they constantly reminded him that he would never be a native, but that was fine with him.

Come January, he had to take inventory. He was making a modest profit but saw possibilities and growth in the town. Soon the storekeeper was becoming accepted, for they liked the way he was doing business. He had disposed of the old stock at a sacrifice and was concerned that he had made a poor showing.

In addition to the selling products in the country store, he also needed to find store furnishings, displays and fixtures. At good antique stores, flea markets and the like, the storekeeper found tasteful country items that would direct the customer to specific items in the store and call up the memories of the store's history.

CREDIT AND BOOKKEEPING

Credit was a problem from the previous owner, for he had left a bad track record with the banks and customers alike. Establishing credit from the banks and wholesale houses and giving credit to his customers seemed to be difficult, but the storekeeper needed to pay the wholesalers in order to keep his good credit and had to collect customer accounts in order to live. When World War II came along, the authorities tightened up, and he was notified that all bills had to be paid within thirty days. The notification was a real kick in the hind-end by a mule, so to speak, and demonstrated a problem between the two kinds of credit. Soon he realized that he had to start a collection campaign with the customers.

Country storekeeping depended on such a variety of collection methods that it was almost impossible to adopt a uniform policy. The merchant could keep his accounts in many different ways before cash registers were available. He could run up a column of figures on shingles, or he might calculate by pictograph, which was quite popular for New Hampshire merchants who got confused about whether the customer owed the storekeeper for the cheese at the time the transaction was recorded. The storekeeper could not escape the burden of accounting for the sold goods and payment. He tried to collect and limit credit to those who would pay in thirty days, but he had to make exceptions nearly every day.

Historian Gerald Carson provides the following experience:

> *James L. Bragg used to run a general store with a lumberyard in the back of it. One day a farmer wanted some cedar shingles. The quantity Bragg had on hand, as it turned out, was just what the customer wanted. "I'll take them all," he said. But Bragg had [him] back-off on the last bundle. "I couldn't sell that one," he explained. "It's got my store accounts on it."*

The country trader usually kept his accounts in great folios, full-sized sheets of white paper folded once by the stationery to make four pages. Each account book was ruled according to its use (for cash, daybook, single or double entry) and could be had for about a dollar and a half. The Yankee Storekeeper found that the best way to keep his record was in a bound book, a "daybook." From such a book a fair copy was made into the ledger, the chronological scribbles arranged as debit and credit items so as to reflect the standing of each customer. To cut down on the work, the items were copied off the ledger. Sometimes only numbers were used, referring back to the page in the journal where the purchases were listed. Further original examples of the daybook records may be found at the end of this book.

The instincts of a good merchant are all toward waiting on customers and promoting trade. Yet the Yankee Storekeeper would find himself toiling over his housekeeping, checking invoices and arranging stock. Hour by hour, he transcribed, posted, totaled and sometimes rectified his mistakes.

Customers would buy a bill of goods and promise to pay it in thirty days, and if they paid in a year, they thought he ought to give them a cigar.

One of his thirty-day customers assured the storekeeper that he could pay. He let him have twenty-five dollars worth of goods, and for a "long

Daybook accounting and charges, November 1831. This portion of daybook page is from an East Moultonborough store owned by Nathaniel V. Shannon and operated by Jonathan Richardson. The store opened for trade on January 27, 1831. *Courtesy of Steve Holden.*

time [he did not] see him." The customer ignored his statements and letters of concern until the storekeeper penned him the following letter:

Dear Sir:

When you asked for credit you promised to pay me in 30 days. You assured me you could do this, if not sooner. Now nine months have passed and I have never seen you or heard from you. I realize you may be hard up. I know what it is to be hard up as anyone in the past, but when I owed a bill and couldn't pay it as I agreed, I always wrote my creditor and explained the situation and told him just what I could and I never had any trouble. Now you don't answer my letters and your promises are no good. I am going to make you a promise. If I don't hear from you by next Saturday I will sue you on Monday, and if you don't believe I keep my promise, just wait until Monday.

On Saturday, a young lady came in and handed the proprietor a letter. It contained four pages of abuse, but it had twenty-five dollars in it. He receipted the bill and closed the book. The storekeeper felt that he had lost a customer, but he had received his money. The next Thursday, however, in came the man and warmed his hands at the stove. The storekeeper thought, "He'll wait till I see him, and then go and trade with my competitor to make me feel bad." At that point, the storekeeper disappeared out the back door to deprive him the satisfaction. Later he returned just in time to see him loading a very large order of food goods in his wagon. He had bought about forty dollars worth and paid cash. As it turned out, the man owed almost every storekeeper in town except him.

Credit is sometimes difficult to figure out, but the storekeeper had always observed that honest intentions are the second-best thing to honest actions.

The storekeeper was approached one day by a young man who wanted a pair of pants for himself and a pair of shoes for his lady friend. He claimed he was working at the sawmill and would pay for the goods on Saturday when he got his pay.

The storekeeper soon found out he was a liar. The man had never worked for the sawmill and had no property. The storekeeper did some serious studying on the case and came up with an effective action that has given good results many times.

In a nearby town was a collection agency that had a reputation for meaning business. One storekeeper informed the agency that he had a bill to collect from a man who had died and wished it to be attached to the man's casket. The action held up the funeral until the outraged family collected the amount for the bill. The proprietor wrote the following letter to the collection agency:

Dear Sir:

This particular customer (nameless) got these goods from me by lying. This brings him under the statute for getting goods under false pretenses. Now I want you to have him arrested at once, and I will make a case against him that will keep him in prison for a couple of years. I don't care about the cost. I want to hang him up like a crow in the cornfield to scare the others.

The letter was signed, put into an envelope and addressed, as if by error, to the unnamed customer. The next morning when he opened the store, an old woman sat on the steps. She said, "I want to pay a bill that my son owes, and I want a receipt in full." She got it and probably is still wondering why the lightning never struck.

The 1880s saw the beginning of the end for the old methods of bookkeeping. The first cash register was making its appearance in the old store. The register recorded all transactions that occurred between storekeeper and customer. It saved time, labor and bookkeeping. The register appealed to the eye with a shiny nickel beauty and to the ear with a pleasant *bong* when the lever was passed. Like the automobile, it had an audiovisual, mechanical charm.

Major Changes in the Old Country Store

During the 1860s, a few articles were made ready-wrapped of a convenient size for the customer, and on the wrapping was the brand as an identifying label. For example, "Robert Burns" was a cigar name. Another example was "Chas. H. Fletcher's Castoria," which was in a labeled bottle. The use of the trademark names gradually drew the attention of the buyer, and the practice was quickly accepted. In 1870, there were only a handful of registered trademarks, but widespread changes took place beginning in the 1890s through the early 1900s when products came to the store individually wrapped in tin containers, paper boxes, sealed bags and bottles, all carrying eye-appealing labels.

The old coffee grinder survived in the country store for a long time before it became obsolete and was replaced by convenient packaging. You may find these old coffee grinders in antique stores today.

As manufacturers began to see that packaging was not only a fine container of goods but also a sales builder, attractive labels were applied to the products. The Indian motif as displayed at the country stores not only led to cigar store sculpture but also gave the image that was displayed on cigar boxes.

Carson records the following in his *Old Country Store*:

> *When we remember that the nineteenth-century merchant was the dominant figure in commerce rather than the manufacturer, it is not surprising to find that the retailer, not the maker, did the advertising. Until deep into the century, most advertisers were content to announce that certain goods had arrived, for it was a greater feat to acquire a stock than to sell it.*
>
> *The historic change in merchandising methods, from the twilight confusion of the old cracker barrel store to the disciplined brightness and order of the modern shopping center began when factories packed their first consumer units—a "paper" of coffee, a "paper" of years—and shipped them twenty-four or thirty-six to the case, in wooden boxes.*
>
> *As recently as the 1900's, when a factory manager pushed back his "Kelly" and picked up his trade paper, Packages, he could find in it a modest department called "Paper Box News."*

Packaging and labeling the goods took away the salesmanship of the proprietor of the store. Slowly the merchant gave up the old mercantilist philosophy of buy low and sell high and turned to the idea of selling the largest possible volume of goods, faster than ever before and at a lower margin of profit.

It was during the early 1920s that business started slowing down though the change had been coming for a while. The old cracker barrel days ended as early as the 1890s when the National Biscuit Company packed its Unseeded Soda Crackers in a family-sized, moisture-proof pack. Cheese wheels declined after Kraft developed processed cheese, packaged in small family-sized containers. Soon fruit sales fell off and to-go orders for food declined. The packaged goods and similar commodities had taken over, especially the three-minute, easy-to-prepare food. Families had changed their habits.

The Yankee Storekeeper saw his country store business falling off and knew the old days would never return. Some old stores retained some of their nostalgia and bygone features, but they were dying out, and shop owners knew it.

Our proprietor made a good living in the store business, and he might pass on some words of wisdom and possibly encourage a new owner to take over the store. A nameless proprietor in New Hampshire made the following observation:

> *It's too bad I can't keep on as a Yankee Storekeeper—it's been a lot of fun. But the gasoline and wood business has its amusing moments, too, and every once in a while I get a chance to use to advantage the tricks I've learned from my father on the farm, from my customers in the store, and from the smart city folks determined to sell me a pile of goods big enough to choke a horse.*

RUNNING THE STORE—A FAMILY AFFAIR

The novelty, nostalgia and pure pleasure of reviving the old traditions of the country store is still fun.

Once again the country dealer has to adjust to new conditions in order to operate a family country store. Everything appears easy, but business is much faster. The store itself looks brighter, neater and more inviting. Everyone seems happier except the checkerboard strategist—who is no longer granted the solace of a free cracker—the dog who could not get at the Leaf Lard and perhaps the owner himself.

There are fewer of those weekend night orders to put up for the families because smaller farms are producing larger crops and buying their supplies where stocks are larger and prices lower.

On an average day, you might find the lady of the store weighing goods, sweeping, grinding the coffee and serving the customers who stop in daily to pick up their mail and staples and enjoy some good conversation over a cup of coffee.

The Yankee Storekeeper had to decide what he needed to order to keep his shelves well stocked with the essentials and novelty items that drew the customers to the store.

The storekeeper also had to have a good sense of arithmetic. He kept track of what everyone owed him in the town. He had to be careful that people didn't cheat him. He was sometimes a postmaster because the post office was often found in the store. He had to know how much postage to charge on

At the store counter are the clerk, proprietor and customer. *Courtesy of Stephen J. Voormies.*

incoming letters and packages. To many of his customers, he was the town banker and lawyer. He would advise people on deals, help with contracts and sign or co-sign contracts. The storekeeper also issued marriage licenses.

Often, the storekeeper made frequent trips to the city for supplies. While there, he learned of new products, fashions and ways of doing business in order to keep up with new trends. He also brought the news back to the village. In earlier days, the newspaper was not delivered from door to door. Most of the time, depending on the town, only one copy of the paper was available for the community to share, and the paper was found in the store.

Another important responsibility of the storekeeper was that he had to be careful not to offend his customers. He always had to be a good diplomat and careful not to turn his back on the customer, and by all means the storekeeper did not embarrass his customers. It was most important to be friendly, and the more friendly he was the more the customers would want to go to his store. He had to realize that most families were self-sufficient; they did not have to make many trips to the store because they could make almost everything they needed at home. If the country store were fun to visit and the proprietor friendly, people wanted to make more trips to the store, for then it was the magnet of the town and a pleasant place to visit.

The storekeeper's children usually worked in the store, preparing for the day when they would be the storekeepers. Some of their chores would include sweeping out the store, unloading and loading the farmers' wagons, polishing the brass, weighing scales and dusting the shelves. The biggest job of the week was helping to prepare for Saturday, the busiest shopping day. With much of the food at the store stored in bulk, such as the oatmeal contained in large sacks or barrels, plenty of hands were needed to package the food for the many customers as they selected their supplies.

The older children in the family learned to keep the accounts of the business. When their father went on a business trip, they would carry on the daily business as acting storekeepers.

ADVERTISING

A word to the wise: if you are interested in opening your own country store, you might want to have a few old containers and a few pieces of advertising in the storeroom. Now that the old country stores are becoming very popular and intriguing, old store paraphernalia is appearing more in auctions, antique shops, secondhand stores, antique shows and flea markets.

II
MISCELLANEOUS STORE FIXTURES

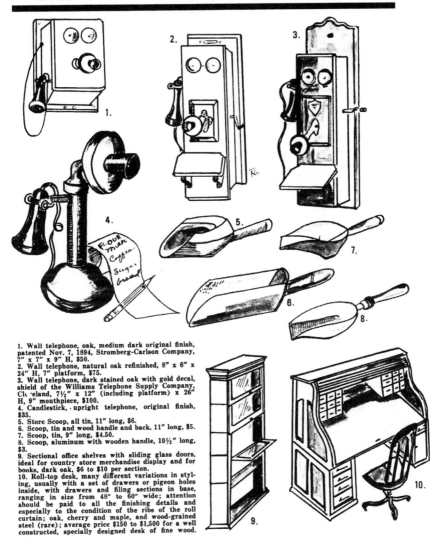

1. Wall telephone, oak, medium dark original finish, patented Nov. 7, 1894, Stromberg-Carlson Company, 7" x 7" x 9" H, $50.
2. Wall telephone, natural oak refinished, 8" x 6" x 24" H, 7" platform, $75.
3. Wall telephone, dark stained oak with gold decal, shield of the Williams Telephone Supply Company, Cleveland, 7½" x 12" (including platform) x 26" H, 9" mouthpiece, $100.
4. Candlestick, upright telephone, original finish, $35.
5. Store Scoop, all tin, 11" long, $6.
6. Scoop, tin and wood handle and back, 11" long, $5.
7. Scoop, tin, 9" long, $4.50.
8. Scoop, aluminum with wooden handle, 10½" long, $3.
9. Sectional office shelves with sliding glass doors, ideal for country store merchandise display and for books, dark oak, $6 to $10 per section.
10. Roll-top desk, many different variations in styling, usually with a set of drawers or pigeon holes inside, with drawers and filing sections in base, ranging in size from 48" to 60" wide; attention should be paid to all the finishing details and especially to the condition of the ribs of the roll curtain; oak, cherry and maple, and wood-grained steel (rare); average price $150 to $1,500 for a well constructed, specially designed desk of fine wood.

This would be a typical example of store fixtures, phones and so on. *Courtesy of Roselyn Grossholz.*

If you keep your eyes open, sometimes these items may be found on farms in tool sheds, barns and workshops or in the basements, attics, garages and tool sheds of old houses. Other places to look include old hotels, drugstores, wholesale food stores, tobacco shops and old warehouses.

There are a lot of nostalgic items that may be found in old country stores. In many of the legitimate old stores, advertising material in the form of signs, posters, calendars, trading cards and fixture displays are a must. Commercially, old store material lends itself to decorating, especially in antique stores, restaurants and clothing stores. A personal collection of store material may be used to decorate a home.

The local country store is an innovative and provocative museum exhibition that will, and should, influence customers from all walks of life. Many new owners have enjoyed restoring the old by renewing a historic house. Regardless of where, when or how often we frequent the country store, these small vanishing vestiges of enterprise still remain a shared experience not to be quickly forgotten.

Our remaining country (general) stores survive only because we care and want to preserve our heritage—and perhaps a little because we wish to reminisce over the "good old days."

Chapter 5

The Old Country Stores of
New Hampshire

The following are representative histories of the old country stores in New Hampshire. Many of these histories have been provided for use in this book by past and present proprietors. By good authority, these country stores have met the criteria and standards of the classic country and general stores of New Hampshire. Unfortunately, many of these stores are no longer in existence, but we will attempt to present a representation of their legacy.

THE BRICK STORE, BATH, 1790

Mike and Nancy Lusby, Proprietors

According to the owners, Mike and Nancy Lusby, The Brick Store is the oldest continuously operated general store in the United States and is appropriately listed in the National Register of Historic Places. The following history is given by the owners:

> *The Brick Store is a genuine, old-fashioned general store that dates back as far as 1790. Although nothing can compare to actually visiting the store in Bath and experiencing the sights, sounds and smells that greet you there, we hope you will enjoy clicking your way through our electronic store.*
>
> *Having served as the post office until 1942, some of the original post office boxes still remain. On the outside brick walls you may still see the old painted signs advertising Morrison's English Liniment and Lady Poor's*

An appropriate scene of the country store that may have been seen in New Hampshire during the early 1900s. Note the fox resting in the lower right of the picture. *Courtesy of Greg Heppe.*

The Brick Store, Route 302, located in the village of Bath, circa 1790. *Courtesy of Mike and Nancy Lusby.*

The Brick Store was built between 1790 and 1804. The Brick Store is America's oldest continuously run general store. *Courtesy of author's collection.*

Ointment. Inside the store the front of the old counters are slanted to allow the ladies with their hoop skirts to step up close to inspect the merchandise in the display cases.

The Village of Bath is a must-stop destination—a small piece of Americana where you can spend hours browsing the Brick Store, cooling off with a sundae at the ice cream shop, browsing through an art gallery, or relaxing on the deck overlooking the picturesque Ammonoosuc River and the Bath Covered Bridge, one of three covered bridges in the area.

Those of you familiar with the Brick Store will recognize our products and down-home atmosphere. The Brick Store will take you back to the eighteenth century and celebrate the romance and nostalgia of early New Hampshire.

Mike and Nancy Lusby bought the Brick Store in 1992, leaving California commuting behind and opting for the beauty and serenity of life in New Hampshire's White Mountains. Mike's brother Jim is indispensable as the Store Manager. Their son Michael, and daughter Mindy and Shannyn help round out this family operation.

The store is located on Route 302 in the village of Bath, New Hampshire.

CALEF'S COUNTRY STORE, BARRINGTON, 1869
Greg Bolton, Proprietor

When you come to New Hampshire, this is a "must" visit. As with most country stores in the Granite State, the reception is warm and sincere—a welcome into the 1800s and a unique journey into the past that will be remembered for many years.

Calef's Country Store has been a New Hampshire tradition since 1869. There is a very interesting history to this store, which is given by the owner Greg Bolton:

In 1869, Mary Chesley Calef mortgaged the farm and added a modest sum that she had earned as a teacher. She then defied the traditional notion of where "a woman's place is" by opening a store right in the front room of her home.

Like most country stores of her time, it stocked a little of everything— molasses carted by oxen, firkins of lard, hogsheads of vinegar, salt fish

Calef's Country Store, Barrington Village, circa 1869. *Courtesy of Greg Bolton.*

Calef's Country Store has been a New Hampshire tradition since 1869. Today it attracts many visitors still. *Courtesy of author's collection.*

from Gloucester and crackers in barrels. Her son, Austin, took over after her death in 1907, For the next forty years, the store continued to serve the local community, even as he was a senator for six years (1933–9). The Calef family continued Mary's standard of quality and service for five generations.

Walk through the door of the store today and be transported back to a simpler time in life. The floors creak with stories, the wood stove warms the passersby and the smell of homemade bread and donuts entice even the healthiest of folks. Jars and jars of penny candy delight children of all ages. Homemade jams and jellies, pickles in the barrels and the famous Snappy Old Cheese keep customers coming year round.

The store is located at 606 Franklin Pierce Highway, in the village of Barrington, New Hampshire.

THE CARDIGAN COUNTRY STORE, BRISTOL, 1800s
Steven and Nancy Bleiler, Proprietors

This old building, which houses the country store, was built in 1800 by John Sleeper. According to Richard W. Musgrove's 1923 *History of Bristol*, it was the seventh-oldest building in Bristol and known as the Old Tannery building.

In 2011, the Bleiler family, who own and operate the Cardigan Mountain Orchards in Alexandria, New Hampshire, decided to purchase the tannery building and restore it as a country store. One year later, the Bleilers have done just that. Their stock features a full line of general merchandise, fancy dry goods and gifts of all kinds made especially for the discriminating New England customer. This "old time" country store replicates the nostalgia of the early country store. This unique store is well stocked with bric-a-brac of old household goods. It is an emporium of creative American wares. From old fashion to new, they have it at this country store.

The Bleilers are now in the process of extending the building to house a fully equipped historical museum depicting a tasteful collection of farm and household antiques.

The Bleilers' three sons are also active in the project of restoring the old heritage of the town with its country store. They are William, Stephen and David Bleiler.

Cardigan Country Store is located on Main Street in Bristol, New Hampshire. Originally the building was considered the seventh-oldest building in Bristol and was known as the Old Tannery building, circa 1800s. *Courtesy of author's collection.*

The Bleiler family purchased the building and successfully transformed it into a typical old country store. Visitors are seen making purchases at the store's counter. *Courtesy of author's collection.*

The store is located on Main Street in the village of Bristol, New Hampshire.

The Common Man Company Store, Ashland, 1996

Diane Downing, Proprietor

Carole Palmer, Manager

Erica Auciello Murphy, director of communication and community relations for the Common Man Company, presents the following history:

> *The Common Man Company Store opened in 1996 and was the brainchild of Diane Downing, partner in the Common Man family of restaurants.*
>
> *In the early Common Man days, Diane offered a variety of Common Man goods in an old cupboard at the host desk at the Ashland restaurant. The popularity of this little "store" paved the way for the opening of The Common Man Company Store, right across the street from the restaurant.*
>
> *What was once a post office became a two-story country store with signature items from the Common Man, such as logo t-shirts and gear, mugs, soup mix, wine, jams, salsa and the restaurant's famous white chocolate. Diane aims to offer useful and fun products including house ware, kitchen gadgets, candles and cookbooks, as well as New Hampshire items. The children's section is full of wonderful old-fashioned games, crafts, books and plush animals. A personal care section offers a variety of lotions and soaps made by New Hampshire vendors.*
>
> *The Common Man Company Store's trademark homemade fudge has become a staple with guests. Adults and children alike enjoy the ten-foot penny candy counter that is filled with old-time nostalgic goodies alongside new favorites.*

The store is located on Main Street in Ashland, New Hampshire.

Ashland Common Man Company Store is prominently seen on Main Street in the village of Ashland, New Hampshire. *Courtesy of author's collection.*

THE CRACKER BARREL, HOPKINTON, 1793

Paul and Marilyn McGuire, Proprietors

For more than three centuries this well-known general store has resided in the village of Hopkinton, New Hampshire. The store began as an old country store with a variety of household goods, general merchandise, dry goods, patent medicine and numerous other sundries; however, over the years its specialty has been concentrated as a grocery store featuring the finest meats and produce.

The store is highly rated and worth the trip to experience a fine old village store. It is located at 377 Main Street, Hopkinton, New Hampshire.

Cracker Barrel, 377 Main Street Hopkinton, New Hampshire. The traditional country store is considered a magnet for the village of Hopkinton, circa 1793. *Courtesy of author's collection.*

THE SANDWICH GENERAL STORE, SANDWICH, 1800S

By the 1870s this area was already a thriving business and social center of the town. The country store was the heart of the community.

According to the Sandwich Historical Society, the following is written about the history of Sandwich:

> *In 1945, the general store, next to the post office, was purchased by Nick Floyd. Roger and Martha Deming lived on the second floor and ran the store for ten years.*

The eighteenth and nineteenth annual excursions of the Sandwich Historical Society indicate what might have been seen on a walk around the center in 1850s:

> *An apothecary shop and a pharmacy, a bank, three blacksmiths, two cabinets shops, two coffin shops, four general stores, a harness shop, a hotel, four mills and a tannery, one millinery and a tailor shop, a house painter, three physicians' offices, two shoemaking establishments, five shoe shops, a tavern, two tinsmiths, an upholstery store and a wheelwright.*

Located in Center Sandwich Village, New Hampshire, the Sandwich General Store was a thriving center of the town, circa 1800s. *Courtesy of author's collection.*

Today, the store stands empty, just waiting for a new proprietor. *Courtesy of author's collection.*

The general store, like most of the country stores in New Hampshire, was closed due to the lack of business. Today, it is vacant. The store is located in the village of Sandwich, New Hampshire.

D.D. GILCHRIST GENERAL STORE, FRANKLIN, 1815

D.D. Gilchrist, Proprietor

A dealer in groceries, dry goods, notions, boots and shoes crockery and glassware, this general store had a heavy stock of general merchandise always on hand. More than forty-five years after it was opened, Mr. Gilchrist became a partner in 1860 and gained sole proprietorship by 1879. Mr. Gilchrist's long experience and very favorable relations with producers enabled him to quote the lowest market rates in every department of his business.

DODGE'S GENERAL STORE, NEW BOSTON, 1872

Sam and Manisha Patel, Proprietors

Dodge's General Store is considered the centerpiece of the village of New Boston. This historic red building has graced the village since 1872 and continues its tradition as the gathering place for business and social matters of the town.

The store fell into hard times and was sold at auction to Sam and Manisha Patel at a reasonable price. Manisha Patel said that she bought the business because she needed a project to keep her busy and loved the general store in town, so she immediately hired local tradesmen and craftsmen to whip the store into shape.

Soon after it was restored, local patrons and visitors arrived in the village and would stop for a loaf of bread or a cup of coffee. They found a store that, though spruced up and freshly painted, wasn't a whole lot different from how it was before—warm, cordial and most inviting. The countertops have been refurbished, the tin ceiling sparkles and the old sign hangs above the door.

Most of the people who were working at Dodge's when it closed returned to their old jobs, including Debbie Smith, the store manager.

This is a good-sized general store, and many of the local people tend to stop by it, and other mom and pop stores like it, to grab a bite to eat.

The store sells the customary groceries, convenience items, newspapers, cold drinks, freshly brewed New England Coffee and a selection of baked goods. It also servers prepared food items and ready-made salads from Mike's Red Bark, located in Salem.

On a personal note, I spent many enjoyable years at Dodge's store in my youth. I marched in the Fourth of July parades in the village during the '40s and enjoyed the outdoor movies at the ballpark on Saturday evening. When I went into the store, I was fascinated with the many varieties of items that were displayed throughout the store. There were colorful posters and advertisements, toys, tools, kitchen goods, groceries, cider, pickle and cracker barrels, farm equipment and, most importantly, the penny candy counter, where the jawbreakers were located. There was no end to the goodies in the store.

Fadden's General Store and Maple Sugarhouse, North Woodstock, 1896

Jim Fadden, Proprietor

In 1896, the Fadden family chose North Woodstock in the White Mountains to settle and establish a general store and a maple sugarhouse business. Five generations of the Faddens have not only run their own general store but also harvested maple sap and produced syrup and sugar.

Fadden's General Store became the center of town activity and, like most country stores, was considered a popular gathering place for social, political and town business.

When you enter the store, the clerk greets you, and you find yourself surrounded with the fragrance of leather, tobacco, boots and the aroma of spices. Looking to the left as you enter the store, you will see displayed a large moose head hanging on a post and below it, a large, Round Oak no. 20 black parlor stove that sets the proper atmosphere for the store. Looking to the right, you will see the customary long wooden and glass counter display, well stocked with tasteful gifts and New Hampshire–made souvenirs.

The store is well stocked with a full line of general merchandise, tobacco, sundries, souvenirs, camping supplies, groceries and dairy products, as well as its signature maple syrup. An added attraction to the store is the sugarhouse museum with displays of town and store history.

Fadden's General Store and Maple Sugarhouse, Main Street, North Woodstock, New Hampshire. This photograph was taken in August 1926 during Old Home Day. Far left with his arms crossed is Norman Fadden, and on the far right with the apron is Ida Fadden. The man standing at the top of the stairs with the white shirt and tie is James H. Fadden. *Courtesy of Jim Fadden.*

Fadden's General Store as it appears today on Main Street in North Woodstock. *Courtesy of Jim Fadden.*

The store is well known for preserving the heritage of the old general store. As you leave, you know that you had stepped into the past and experienced an old country store in the Granite State. The romance of the early country store is still alive in North Woodstock. Stop in and say hello. The store is located on the Main Street, North Woodstock, New Hampshire.

THE FREEDOM VILLAGE STORE, FREEDOM, 1860
Miranda Sandahl, Proprietor

Historian Edward S. Leonard gives the following history of the Village Store:

The 1860 map identifies "Elias Towne Store" at this location. The three-story structure with mansard roof drawn here may date from 1875. Operators of the store included Ralph Foster after 1890, Arthur Tilton after 1929, and later Albert Whittaker.

The store carried clothing, shoes, groceries and later, gasoline. Everett and Betty Nichols and Barney and Ruth Jones succeeded these owners. After that the store was run by a succession of short-term owners including Bennett Goldstein.

Renamed the Freedom Country Store in 1984, groceries, gasoline, souvenirs and sandwiches were sold until 1989 when the store closed. The gasoline pumps were removed in 1994.

Reopened in 1999 as the Freedom Village Store, antiques, greeting cards, flowers and gifts were sold. At that time Pamela Clemons-Keith was the owner and manager.

In 2009, the store was operated by volunteer citizens of the town and managed by Miranda Sandahl.

Freedom Village Store, Freedom, New Hampshire. Originally, this location was known as the Elias Towne Store, circa 1860. *Courtesy of author's collection.*

W.A. Gardner & Company General Merchandise, Tilton, 1887

W.A. Gardner, Proprietor

For the duration of the store's operations, which began in 1887, "all sales were made at the lowest price for cash." The stock included a complete assortment of fine staples and fancy groceries, crockery, china and glassware, and the goods were selected expressly for family trade. The teas, coffees and spices were advertised as being of "exceptional purity" and with a "delicacy of flavor."

Mr. Gardner, a native of Franklin, was well known in the vicinity. He was known to have given close attention to the filling of orders and to have employed sufficient assistance with his promise of prompt, courteous and accurate service to each and every customer. This was truly a general store of quality.

The store was located on Main Street, Tilton, New Hampshire, but is no longer in business.

Golden Pond Country Store, Holderness, Early 1900s

Steve Merrill, Proprietor

Steven and Lisa Merrill purchased this fine old store from the Chesleys, who owned it from 1991 to 2006. Their intent was to transform the property into a local landmark. In 2007, the old building had a face-lift into an Adirondack-style lodge with the atmosphere of old New Hampshire.

This move was a major change for the family. Steve and Lisa relocated to New Hampshire from Massachusetts. Steve was in sales for a telecommunication equipment company, and Lisa was in charge of a major publishing company. It was certainly worthwhile, for they are now located on the shore of Golden Pond.

The store offers homemade meals and sandwiches, as well as a wide variety of food, gifts and bric-a-brack for the entire family.

The store is located in the village of Holderness, Routes 3 and 25 (by the bridge) on Squam Lake.

Golden Pond Country Store, Routes 3 and 25, at the bridge in Holderness, New Hampshire. Steve Merrill, proprietor, has successfully transformed his country store into a local landmark. *Courtesy of author's collection.*

THE GRAFTON GENERAL STORE (BARNEY'S STORE), GRAFTON, 1840s

Vinny Bianco, Proprietor

Barney's General Store in Grafton Village is the oldest continuously operated store in the town. There have been many proprietors of this fine store during the course of its 125 years. Of these years, the name Barney was associated with the store for more than seventy-five.

In Kenneth R. Cushing's *Isinglass, Timber and Wool: A History of the Town of Grafton, 1761–1992*, the following history of the general store is given:

> *The store's origin can be traced to its founder, Jesse Cass, who at one time owned not only the site upon which the store rests but also much of the land that encompasses the village. During 1849, Jesse Cass was a farmer who owned a considerable amount of land. In 1848, the value of the land that bordered the Smith River rose considerably when the Northern Railroad*

Grafton General Store, 377 Main Street (Route 4), Grafton, New Hampshire. This country store was known as Barney's General Store and known in Grafton Village as the oldest continuously operated store in the town, circa 1840. *Courtesy of author's collection.*

laid its tracks through it. Although Grafton's first depot was located at the Center, additional room for freight and passengers was soon needed by the railroad. Recognizing the potential of his property, Jess sold a lot to the Northern for a depot and freight yard. He then proceeded to develop his land around the railroad's new depot. In 1849, he joined Alfred Barney to establish a store across from the depot.

There is a very interesting story related to the history of the general store that Cushing details in his *History of the Town of Grafton*:

H. Barney and son received a carload of floor from the west, the third carload within the last six months.

There must have been a lot of baking going on in Grafton during those months!

The store offered something for everyone. Like its counterpart, it carried a variety of goods, but the store was a social mecca as well, due to the presence of a hall above the store. The hall featured an anteroom, a large kitchen and a large floor space with a stage at one end. Some of the organizations that met there on a regular bases included the Eureka Grange #69 and the American Mechanics (Order of the United American Men). Special events included school graduations and traveling minstrel shows such as "Old Brag and his medicine show." There was also another floor above the hall that children would visit in order to view through the cracks in the floor the proceedings of Jehovah Witnesses who would sometimes meet in the hall.

On June 20, 1924, Alden Barney passed away. His daughter Verna, declined to carry on the family business. An era had passed. Archie Kimbal of East Grafton and owner of the former E.F. Folsom's store purchased Barney's store. He operated it for four years when he sold it to Grover L. Barney who also ran it for four years until his death. In 1935, Arthur and Lillian Reney purchased the store. A new era was about to begin.

Arthur and Lillian Reney carried on the tradition of running the store and making the hall available for public use. In the late 1940s, Lillian accepted the position of postmaster from Bertha Barney. Accordingly, the post office was moved from the depot to a corner of the store, which it had occupied some years earlier. For close to twenty years the Reney's waited on customers. During the Reneys' tenure, one story stands out that typifies Arthur's wit. What storekeeper has not heard at one time or another that his prices are too high? Arthur had a ready retort when he was confronted with such a complaint. When a fellow walked into his store and asked for the price of a pair of overshoes displayed on a shelf, Arthur told the fellow that they were selling for twelve dollars. "Why," the fellow replied, "I can buy the same pair of overshoes from Sears & Robuck for ten dollars!" To this statement Arthur observed that an order from Sears would take three weeks to fill, but in all fairness, the fellow would sell the overshoes for the same price. Delighted in having struck a bargain, the fellow whipped out his money, and handed it to Arthur who promptly turned away without handing over the overshoes. The perplexed fellow then testily asked, "Where are my overshoes?" Arthur replied, "They will be ready in three weeks!"

In 1955 Arthur Reney passed away, his widow sold the store to a young couple from Texas, John and Edna Gordon. The Gordons adapted the store to a rapidly changing world. They rearranged the interior, replacing many of the time worn cabinets and shelving. The store's inventory was gradually changed to accommodate the changing demands of the public. No longer was Grafton a self-sufficient, agricultural community. Groceries and ready-made clothing were more in demand. The character of the store was gradually evolving from a general to a convenience store.

Hunting season brought more business to the store. The postwar years saw a steady drove of city dwellers flocking to the country to hunt. John would open the store at six in the morning to supply a crowd of hunters with ammunition, clothing and assorted paraphernalia. He also ran a deer checking station. Anywhere from fifty to seventy-five deer would be checked into the station during hunting season.

When discount stores opened in Lebanon, many of Gordon's customers began to shop there. With the completion of Interstate 89, much of the through traffic fell off. Eventually the meat counter was discontinued and the clothing department closed until the store came to offer only convenience items such as beer, gasoline and snacks. The Gordons weathered these changes, which had closed many of Grafton's other stores. For a time Gordon's was the only store in Grafton. In 1998, they sold the store to another couple, Joe and Eleanor Thomas who operated the store.

Today, the proprietor of this fine general store is Vinny Bianco. The Grafton General Store is located on 377 Main Street (Route 4), Grafton, New Hampshire.

HARMAN'S CHEESE & COUNTRY STORE, SUGAR HILL, 1955
Maxine and Brenda Aldrich, Proprietors

The following excerpts have been taken from the advertising flyer that was written for the customer to enjoy about Harman's Country Store's history:

In 1954, John and Kate Harman retired from life in New York and bought a small general store in Sugar Hill to start a mail order business. Cheese was their business, so Mr. Harman bought a half ton of aged cheddar cheese and started his "World's Greatest Cheddar Cheese" tradition. This move was no mistake, for they sell over twelve tons of Harmon's Really-Aged Cheddar each year.

The Harmon's loved their customers and their business—always enjoying chatting with them personally. Should a customer be dissatisfied, a

Harmon's Cheese & Country Store, 1400 Route 117, Sugar Hill, New Hampshire. Sugar Hill is a beautiful village located in the heart of the White Mountains. This is a must-visit, charming country store, circa 1955. *Courtesy of author's collection.*

replacement or refund was offered. The customer came first with John and Kate Harmon.

The Harmon's passed away in 1980 after long and fruitful lives and twenty-six years in Sugar Hill. Maxine Aldrich had been working for the Harmon's since 1974; she and her husband Bert became the owners of Harmon's Cheese and Country Store in 1981.

Bert was a resident of Sugar Hill all of his life, being a descendent of the first settlers who arrived in 1780. I came from Vermont to work at the former Hotel Look-off during my college summers. I married Bert in 1955 and moved to his family home in 1956 where I still live.

Sugar Hill is a beautiful community located in the heart of the White Mountains. Many visitors enjoy coming to Sugar Hill during the four seasons of the year for hiking, sledding and skiing in the nearby ski resorts, particularly Cannon Mountain.

The little red store is inviting and is quietly nestled in Sugar Hill village. A special trip to the country store would certainly be worth the while, and it is open year round.

The store is located at 1400 Route 117, Sugar Hill, New Hampshire.

THE HARRISVILLE GENERAL STORE, HARRISVILLE, 1838

This general store is a constant reminder of the Greek Revival period in architecture. It is the most prominent building in the village.

Historian John Border Armstrong recorded the following in an article in the *New Hampshire Sentinel* ("Factory Under the Elms, a History of Harrisville, New Hampshire"):

> *The building was built of red brick, two-and-a-half stories, with a gabled end at the front. If Cyrus Harris did build it, he had little or nothing to do with running it as a store. In 1842, one William Hyde in Harrisville offered his business and stock (but apparently not the building) for sale, "on account of illness," (NHS, January 26, 1842). Two years later another notice appeared in the Sentinel, advertising a "New Store and New Goods at Harrisville." The storekeeper added a note that reveals another home industry of the nineteenth century: "Palm leaf will be furnished to Braiders, and good hats taken in exchange for Goods at fair price" (NHS, May 1, 1844).*
>
> *The operation of the store continued to change hands every few years, and its storekeepers included the D.W. Clements who tangled with Milan Harris in 1856, who own the store during these years. The Cheshire Mills, owned it in 1860, but the Colony's business apparently did not run, or wish to run, a "company store" in the usual sense of the word. When the store came on the market, they sometimes took it over for a period of time and sold, leased or rented it as they could.*

During the early 1900s, the transportation industry felt the effect of an economic decline, and similarly displaced by the automobile, the railroad finally stopped running through Harrisville in 1936:

> *Stores and shops declined in number and variety from the hay day [sic] of the eighties but held their own during the lean times. The increasing numbers*

Harrisville General Store, 29 Church Street, Harrisville, New Hampshire circa 1838. The store, with its Greek Revival architecture, majestically welcomes visitors to enjoy a traditional landmark of New Hampshire's history. *Courtesy of the Historic Harrisville Inc.*

of summer people helped our local stores as indicated in the Sentinel as the following from Chesham: "Bemis Bros., our grocery men, have done a rushing business the past week filling orders for summer residents who are about to open their houses for the summer season. An order, amounting to $75, was received and delivered one day last week to a single family." Then as such things came into use, up-to-date proprietors might add to their stores a soda fountain or gas pump to attract customers.

As the community grew, so, too, did the general store. Town historian Jeannie Eastman reminds us:

The General Store remains a popular meeting place as well as provid[ed] a needed service to local residents. In its early days it was a typical general store, selling kerosene lamps, suspenders, window glass and shoes. It extended credit to customers who settled their debts on payday, and it even supplied the town government with food for tramps in the local tramp house.

Several years ago, Historic Harrisville Inc., the nonprofit foundation that owns the mill buildings, purchased the store. It renovated the interior

This beautiful old red brick building, the most prominent building in historic Harrisville, is seen today welcoming visitors to shop and have a fine lunch. It is hard to imagine visiting Harrisville without making a stop at the general store. *Courtesy of author's collection.*

to include a café, and the business reopened under private ownership after being closed for a decade. Conscious of the store's place in town history, and its role in community life today, Historic Harrisville restarted the business in 2008 when the proprietor decided to leave.

As in the old days, the store registers the pulse of the town. It is the everyday meeting place for residents and visitors where one may encounter selectmen, children leaving the bus stop, business tenants from the mill, the librarian grabbing coffee on her way to work, retired couples enjoying lunch out and telecommuters at their laptops. The store reflects life in the twenty-first century with the ambiance of old world surroundings.

From *New Hampshire Seasons* magazine from fall 2003, Cliff Ann Wales renders the following excerpts from a visit to the Harrisville General Store:

It's hard to imagine visiting Harrisville without making a stop at the general store. It is situated at 29 Church Street on a small hill facing the mills across the canal. Easy to find for travelers, hikers and bicyclists or anyone looking for a bite to eat served up with a lot of local color.

After touring Harrisville and admiring the history, architecture and beauty of the spot, I took some time out to visit the general store. It's a towering old building with several granite steps leading to the refurbished white columned front porch which is outfitted with tables and chairs, just right for enjoying lunch and the fine autumn weather.

To enter the Harrisville General Store you pass through a banging screen door, which announces your arrival. Inside, the store delivers just what you'd expect from a general store: honesty. The spacious wood interior is decorated with black and white photos of local scenes, cheese wheel display, antiques and collectables from the owner's personal cache. Management has created a friendly environment for customers using an old kitchen table and some mismatched chairs that beckon customers to stay awhile and order from the café menu.

To discover what puts this general store in a class by itself, you have to eat or try take-out from the menu. The café serves a wide array of pizzas, burritos, soups, ice cream sandwiches, pastas and granola.

The store is located on 29 Church Street, Harrisville, New Hampshire, and offers the best sandwiches I have ever eaten.

THE HEBRON VILLAGE STORE, HEBRON, 1799

In the early days of the town's existence, there was little excess produced on the farms, but the little there was was used to barter for needed items as hard currency was difficult to come by. By necessity farmers were limited to the articles needed to sustain the farm and family, and for these, they bartered their maple sugar, corn and other crops. It was customary for the local farmer to trade his hay, wood and labor at the Hebron Village Store or in Bristol. The account books for the store from the mid-nineteenth century still exist, and within their pages, everything imaginable that could be produced on the farm was bartered for life's necessities.

During the heyday of the 1880s, the early Hebron general store was well supplied with all the necessities for the local families. However, time took its toll, and the larger chain and grocery stores began to gain popularity. As they became more available to the public, the country store began to lose business.

Hebron Village Store, Hebron Village, New Hampshire, circa 1799. Today, the store is empty and waiting for a new proprietor. *Courtesy of author's collection.*

The store tried several measures to improve business. It traded or bought and sold goods from the farmers, gave credit to them when necessary, started a gift shop, set up luncheon tables and extended its hours, but it had little to no success. To own the store, it was necessary to have a second job.

Today, the store has closed after many years of struggle and countless owners. Unless someone takes up the challenge, the Hebron Village Store, similar to the vacant Center Sandwich General Store, will only become a memory.

The store is located in the village of Hebron, New Hampshire.

ALBERT A. KIDDER & COMPANY GENERAL MERCHANDISE, MEREDITH

Albert A. Kidder, Proprietor

The following excerpt is taken from a advertisement that was published in *Leading Business Men of Meredith* in 1890:

A full line of fancy and family groceries is a prominent feature, the assortment being very complete and being made up of goods that will suit the most fastidious. Particularly is the case as regards teas and coffees, for a specialty is made of these, and the inducements offered are hard to equal, while the prices quoted are remarkably low and indeed it may be said right here that this firm will not be undersold in any department of their business. Boots, shoes and rubbers are dealt in and solid advantages are offered to purchasers of these goods also, the articles being reliable, the style new and popular and the prices low. Whips, etc., are dealt in as are also glass and tin-ware, canned goods, tobacco and cigars and other articles too numerous to mention. This firm makes a specialty of finest cigars and tobacco carrying the largest line and the finest brands of cigars in town, also a complete line of 5, 10, 25 cent goods for household use.

Mr. Kidder built up an extensive trade and won an enviable reputation for enterprise and integrity.

The store was located on Main Street in Meredith Village, New Hampshire. The building is still standing, but the business is closed.

LONG VIEW COUNTRY STORE
Pat and Bill Simon, Proprietors

This beautiful country store is set on a hillside in Meredith that overlooks Meredith and Weirs Bay of Lake Winnipesaukee. The building was originally an early twentieth-century inn, but later in the 1960s, Nancy and Thomas Lindsey bought the building and operated an antique center, known as Burlwood Antique Center starting in the 1970s, out of it. During the 1990s, it was called the Burlwood Country Store.

In February 2004, Pat and Bill Simon bought the property and changed its name to the Long View Country Store—most appropriate for its location. Today, it is one of the finest country stores in the Lakes Region. You name it, they've got it.

The store is located on Route 3 between the Weirs and Meredith Village, New Hampshire.

Long View Country Store, Route 3, Meredith, New Hampshire. The country store has a fantastic view, which looks southeast over Lake Winnipesaukee. *Courtesy of author's collection.*

JOHN MASON GENERAL MERCHANDISE, PLYMOUTH, 1873

John Mason, Proprietor

John Mason founded the store in 1873. In 1876, the firm name became Mason & Weeks. It was again changed in 1879 to Mason, Weeks & Company. In 1886, John Mason came in full control as proprietor.

The store comprises the following:

> *Dry goods, boots and shoes, groceries, flour and grain, paints, and oils, and many other commodities too numerous to mention. All goods were carefully selected and offered at fair prices, which indicates very careful buying and a desire to give customers the full worth of their money in every instance.*

The store was located on Main Street in Plymouth, New Hampshire.

NEW HAMPSHIRE COUNTRY STORE, CHOCORUA, LATE 1700s

Maryanne Canfield, Proprietor

This country store is set in a fully renovated, two-hundred-plus-year-old barn; you will feel welcomed immediately as you enter the front door and step back in time. All three floors are filled with interesting finds, from penny candy, old tin toys and hand-painted glassware to kitchen accessories, home décor, clothing and wrought-iron products.

Like many other country stores in the state, refreshments are served (breakfast and lunch) for the hungry visitor.

The store is located at 229 Route 16 in Chocorua, New Hampshire.

New Hampshire Country Store, 229 Route 16, Chocorua, New Hampshire. The three floors of this store have everything imaginable in an old country store, 1847. *Courtesy of author's collection.*

NORTH SANDWICH COUNTRY STORE, NORTH SANDWICH, 1890S

Michael Shattuck and Lois Carmody, Proprietors

From the archives of the Sandwich Historical Society's publication, the *Fifty-fourth Annual Excursion*, the following account is given:

> *History again changes at the North Sandwich Old Country Store. Mr. and Mrs. Edward Nichols sold the store to Mr. and Mrs. Edgar Merrithew, who have renamed the former country store "Ye Olde Corner Store." They have made many changes and added a fresh meat department. An interesting feature in the store was the enlarged picture taken in 1929 when the store was owned by the late Ansel Lee. In the picture taken in front of the store are Allison Grant, Stanley Quimby and Charles R. Fellows, the model T Ford was Mr. Fellows's.*

The Sandwich Historical Society (1763–1990) reminisced on the store's part in life in Sandwich:

North Sandwich Country Store, 2 Maple Ridge Road, North Sandwich, New Hampshire, circa 1890. *Courtesy of author's collection.*

For many years, Memorial Day was celebrated twice in Sandwich: once in the morning at Ansel Lee's North Sandwich store and again in the afternoon at the Center. The correspondent to the Sandwich Reporter bragged the "the observance at North Sandwich…measured equally with the exercises and crowd at the Center." This rivalry continued into the 1930s with serious checkers competitions between North Sandwich and the Center; when Alsel Lee learned about the ten new pool tables that Everett Merryfield was installing in his store at the Center, Lee promptly ordered a new pool table for his establishment.

Of the four general stores, Albert Kimball's was said to be the finest in Carroll County. No account books remain from any of these tradesmen, but there are the records from Bean's General Store in North Sandwich, which probably are typical. Bean's sold tools, shoes and clothing, cloth, kerosene, tobacco, and a wide variety of food, coffee, eggs, fish, flour, lemons, oats and sugar. The sale of milk does not appear on the records; it must have been purchased directly from the farmer if one didn't own a cow.

North Sandwich Country Store as it appeared in 2012. *Courtesy of author's collection.*

During Alsel Lee's ownership during the early 1900s and through the depression, many good times were celebrated, and good memories are still alive at the North Sandwich store.

In December 1986, the original building burned to the ground. The establishment has been rebuilt, and groceries, delicatessen offerings, hardware supplies and much more may now be found there. It is still called the North Sandwich Country Store and is owned and operated by Lois Carmody and Mike Shattuck.

The store is located in the small village of North Sandwich, New Hampshire.

OLD COUNTRY STORE, MOULTONBOROUGH, 1781

Steve Holden, Proprietor

In the small New Hampshire village of Moultonborough, Freese's Tavern served as the social and political center of the community in the late eighteenth century. In 1793, its owner, George Freese, was issued a tavern and liquor license, and in 1794, he was issued a retailer's license by the town selectmen. Eventually, this building came to be used as a town meeting hall, post office, library and site of trade.

Steve Holden, proprietor of Freese's Tavern's successor, the Old Country Store, provides the following history:

> *The inside of Freese's Store was mostly storage with the trading area to the right of the main floor. This housed a counter, wall shelving, a stove connected to a chimney that was constructed with hand-made bricks and a few oil lamps. On the second floor was a meeting room of George's first tavern.*
>
> *In 1804, the tavern's meeting room was the site of the formal constituting of Morning Star Masonic Lodge by the Grand Lodge of New Hampshire. After the ceremony, the store provided "a rich repast in a style magnificent and splendid" for the Freemasons. The store was then owned by Jonathan Wiggins, a charter member of the Freemasons.*
>
> *Freese was active in town affairs, and in 1816, the town voted to hold its annual meeting at Freese's tavern rather than at the meetinghouse. This arrangement became commonplace during the 1830s, when the tavern was owned by David Bean (1778–1839). Bean, a licensed tavern keeper since*

Old Country Store, Main Street, Moultonborough Corner, Moultonborough, New Hampshire, circa 1781. *Courtesy of author's collection.*

1809, was even more active in public affairs than Freese, and the tavern consequently became more of a focus for town business. In 1831, and almost every year thereafter until Bean's death, town meetings were held at the store. Bean's bar room served as a public meeting place, and legal notices were often posted there as well as at the town meeting house. The tavern also provided a convenient site for auctions and began to assume its present-day role. David Bean became Moultonborough's postmaster in 1837, and the building assumed its future role of post office, a function to which it would return in 1861.

In the year 1851, James French (1811–86), formerly a country merchant in the neighboring community of Tuftonboro, purchased the building and continued his mercantile business there on an enlarged scale until his retirement in 1873, when he was succeeded by his son James E. French, who was a lawyer as well as a merchant and politician.

During the 1850s, items sold and traded in the store were changing. Molasses, rum, sugar, flour and grain by the barrel were still sold in the country stores, but barrels of crackers [and] spices in bulk were not necessarily available by some of the local merchants in the modern convenience stores. Limited amounts of groceries were also available.

In 1861, French was appointed postmaster of Moultonborough. The post office was first located to the left of the building's main entrance, but in the twentieth century [it] *was moved to the attached office at the north corner of the main building where it remained until 1967.*

The frame of the Old Country Store is a two-and-a-half story structure constructed of hand-hewn, full-length timbers, a gable roof and clapboard exterior. Each joint was marked with hand-chiseled Roman numerals, as was each matching brace. On the main building, the roof would have been wooden shingles. The foundation consisted of glacial, granite boulders that were hand-drilled and split by the builders. The foundation was hand-laid and leveled with stone chinking and wedges; no mortar or cement was used. Extending across is a roofed front porch. The store has two brick chimneys, one rising through the front slope of the roof, and the second at the rear of the building near the north corner. Attached to the south elevation of the main building is a shed-roofed wing. It was probably built to shelter horses used on the stagecoaches as well as all horses that passed through town until the turn of the century.

During the 1950s and '60s, this wing was used as a cafeteria and restaurant facility, but today it has been converted over to an extension of the main store.

The main building is intersected by two other wings, which were added during the 1950s. One, a long two-and-a-half story, gable-roofed structure, is attached to the rear of the old wing. This addition is a wide, gable-roofed structure, which also extends to the northwest.

The main building has not changed in proportions and still reveals its origin as a late eighteenth century framed structure. Like many eighteenth century New Hampshire taverns, the Old Country Store contains a combination of semi-public rooms and chambers of types common to domestic structures.

Business within the store is conducted much as it was in earlier times. Sales are not added in [clerks'] *heads but are totaled on the paper bag, and that serves as a receipt. Soda is cooled in the old iceboxes, now refrigerated. Cheese is weighed on a scale patented in 1906. The sales are rung on a brass cash register of about the same age. There is no attempt to sell something that a customer does not want—self-service is the rule or ask if you need help.*

Upstairs in the old meeting room is a museum open to the public at no charge. The focus of the museum is on early life in the area and tools of survival, along with explanations of their use. A roof was added in front of the horse shed to cover the oldest Concord Coach still in existence. The coach was built by the Abbott Company in 1847 for Benjamin Bellows, founder of Bellows Falls, Vermont.

It is interesting to note that there was a stage route that regularly ran from the wharf at Center Harbor to the village of Ossipee and back. From Moultonborough Corner, this route followed the road now called Holland Street to Sandwich Lower Corners, where the Red Brick Store was located, and from there, it took up the old road to Ossipee. Today, there is no stage route or public transportation from these places—the only option for travel between them is through private automobiles on paved roads.

In 1973, the present proprietors of the Old Country Store, Mr. and Mrs. Steve Holden, have tastefully maintained the flavor of the eighteenth-century country store. To enhance the heritage of the store, the Holdens have placed a life-size wooden Indian on the porch of the Old Country Store as a welcome to all visitors to the store. The wooden Indian was carved prior to 1800. On the second floor of the main building is a full-scale historic museum displaying many original artifacts of the period, as well as the town and store's history and heritage.

The Concord Coach was built in 1847. The Concord Coach 22 is the oldest known stagecoach in existence of over three thousand manufactured in Concord, New Hampshire. It was originally built for the Bellows family, founder of Bellows Falls, Vermont. *Courtesy of Steve Holden.*

The Old Country Store in Moultonborough, New Hampshire as it appears today. *Courtesy of Steve Holden.*

The Old Country Store is listed on the National Register of Historic Places under the name of Freese's Tavern.

Today, the store is still an independent family-operated business just as it has been throughout the past 222 years. The Holden family operates the store year round, with daughter Jo as manager.

The store is located on Main Street (Route 25), Moultonborough, New Hampshire.

PHILBRICK & HILL, TILTON, 1871

F.G. Philbrick and J. Hill, Proprietors

The firm of Philbrick & Hill was owned by the prominent men mentioned in this review of Tilton's mercantile enterprise:

> *The original firm name, as adopted in 1871, was J. Hill & F.G. Philbrick, this being changed to the thus present name in 1875. Besides a commodious stock of merchandise, [it] carries a complete stock of hardware, groceries, flour, paint, oils, boots, shoes, rubbers and the standard commodities, including wood. The firm was known for their lowest market prices and dependability of quality.*

The store was located on Main Street, Tilton, New Hampshire.

POLLARD, HARDY & BROWN, DEALER IN GENERAL MERCHANDISE, ASHLAND, 1882

Pollard, Hardy & Brown, Proprietors

This business began in 1882 under the firm name of Pollard, Hardy & Smythe. Its advertisement read as follows:

> *The store is devoted to the sale of dry goods, groceries, hardware, boots, shoes, clothing, paint, oils, etc. Located on additional floors of the building are stocked with furniture, wall paper, curtains, etc. The establishment carried a very fine meat market. The gentlemen are prepared to offer the customer the very best advantages in all the various departments of the business, uniformly in quality and price that can be duplicated by few and excelled by none.*

The store was located on Main Street, Ashland, New Hampshire.

THE RED BRICK STORE, LOWER CORNER, SANDWICH, 1785

Benjamin Burley, Proprietor

The Sandwich Historical Society gives the following record of the Red Brick Store:

> *Before Benjamin Burley opened his store at Lower Corner in 1785, men traveled to the lake on foot, crossed by boat, and walked to Gilmanton, where they bought their supplies, which they carried home on their backs. The second owner of the store was Daniel Little, who operated it for twenty years. The third owner was Arven Blanchard, who ran it for thirty-five years, commencing in the 1940s.*

According to the Sandwich Historical Society (1763–1990), Thomas D. Gotshall moved to Sandwich in the mid-1930s to become postmaster and proprietor of the Lower Corner Grocery and T.D. Gotshall's silver jewelry shop. He proceeded to develop a line of jewelry that was carried on by his son, Abbott, and granddaughter, Mary Ann, and marketed through the

Red Brick Store, Lower Corner, Sandwich, New Hampshire, circa 1785. *Courtesy of author's collection.*

League of New Hampshire Craftsmen, originally known as the League of New Hampshire Arts and Crafts.

The store was located at Sandwich's, Lower Corner, directly across the street from the retirement home of actor Claude Rains. The building is still there but is presently vacant.

ROBIE'S COUNTRY STORE, HOOKSETT, 1887

David and Debra Chouinard, Proprietors

The pulse of the north village was Robie's store, which was the oldest continuously operating business in Hooksett. The store flourished here from the 1800s in the midst of road, river and rail service.

The Historic Preservation Corporation presents the following history:

Robie's Country Store, 9 Riverside Street, Hooksett, New Hampshire, circa 1887. *Courtesy of the Historic Preservation Corporation.*

The original building had a dock facility and received merchandise by river barge until the advent of the railroad in 1842. The building burned in 1857, was rebuilt, burned again in 1906, and was again rebuilt.

George A. Robie bought the store in 1887, and for the next 110 years it was passed down from father to son. The Town of Hooksett considered the store as the social, business, and political center of the community. The store was considered an institution for it supplied the Town of Hooksett with home staples and supplies and also had its own post office.

The last family owner was Lloyd Robie, the fourth generation to operate the store and post office. Lloyd and his wife Dorothy took over the business in March 1965. With their retirement on November 1, 1997, a chapter of New Hampshire history ended.

State, local and presidential candidates found the country store to be a popular stopping spot. Today, it has continued to be very popular for candidates to visit. Many photographs, memorabilia and historic artifacts are tastefully displayed in the museum-like store. The store is known for bringing to life a memorable history of New Hampshire.

Robie's Country Store is a landmark where the town and state's history is being preserved and shared for the general public to appreciate. You will not be disappointed in this experience of the heritage and history of the Granite State that is proudly displayed in the old country store.

The store is located on 9 Riverside Street, Hooksett, New Hampshire.

Rumney Village Store, Rumney, 1865

Ken and Kirstie Savell, Proprietors

Ken Savell, proprietor of the Rumney Village Store, has proudly presented me with the history of the business:

It was founded by Joseph and Sara Abbott in 1865 and was run by them for forty years. The property transitioned to Joseph's son Ira in the 1890s, but the formal transaction was not completed until after Joseph's death when Sarah formally signed it over to Ira in 1912.

Rumney Village Store, Rumney, New Hampshire, circa 1865. *Courtesy of author's collection.*

Ira worked in the store beginning about 1872, and it stayed in the family until 1941 when his widow sold it to George Kelly. Later George Kelly sold it to Anbarth and Ira Anderson during the late '40s early '50s. The Andersons ran the store for approximately twenty years before selling it to the Armitages in 1972.

The Armitages sold the store to Michael and Mary Pope in 1977, and the Popes in turn sold it to the Andrews in 1979. Mark Andrew ran the store for three and a half years before selling it to the Zapletals in 1982. Then Jiri and Tertia Zapletal sold the store to the Giffords after two years in 1984.

The Giffords sold it to Hannigans in 1987. It was then sold to Randy Sampson in 2003, followed by a sale to Deborah Dickman in 2006. After a brief stint of ownership by the Northway Bank, the present owners, Ken and Kirstie Savell, purchased the store in 2010.

A visit to this authentic old New Hampshire village store is certainly worthwhile, for it displays the memorabilia and the general merchandise that you would expect to see in the old country store.

The store is located at 463 Main Street in Rumney, New Hampshire.

THE SHANNON STORE, MOULTONBOROUGH, 1790S

The Moultonborough Historical Society has provided the following history of the Shannon Store:

[Because] *mills were a necessity for settlers, there were many in Moultonborough. Below Birch Hill to the west at a point near where Shannon Brook crosses Route 109, a dam was built with sluices connected to mills below the dam. These included grist, cider, clapboard and shingle mills. Bridges were built across the sluices and that section came to be known as Three Bridges.*

Nathaniel Shannon, one of the original proprietors and owners successfully operated the shingle mill and a store, the foundation of which is still visible. He built a very fine house further along the road.

The store opened for trade on January 27, 1831. No early records are available for the Shannon Store. Additional pages of the daybook are exhibited in chapter six.

Daybook receipts from the Shannon Store, Moultonborough, New Hampshire, early 1800s. *Courtesy of Steve Holden.*

More daybook receipts from the Shannon Store, Moultonborough, New Hampshire, early 1800s. *Courtesy of Steve Holden.*

The store was located at the crossing of the Shannon Brook and Route 109 in Moultonborough, New Hampshire.

TAYLOR & BOND GENERAL STORE, BRISTOL, 1800

I.C. Bartlett, Proprietor

The firm of Taylor & Bond began operations in 1890; however, the business was inaugurated more than half a century earlier by I.C. Bartlett and carried on until 1842. The store was taken up by Bartlett & Taylor until 1859, at which time the business changed hands to Cyrus Taylor and C.G.M. Bond.

The store dealt extensively in general merchandise, and some idea of the magnitude of their business can be obtained in knowing that the store consisted of three spacious floors. The stock included a full line of dry goods, groceries, hardware, hats, caps, carpeting, wallpapers, crockery and glassware.

It was advertised that

> *the quality is as noteworthy as the quantity, for although the firm handles all the standing grades of goods they deal in no articles they cannot guarantee will prove as represented. Bottom prices are quoted in every department of the business, and the employment of four efficient assistants enables orders to be promptly and accurately filled.*

The store was located on Main Street in Bristol, New Hampshire.

THE TUFTONBORO GENERAL STORE, CENTER TUFTONBORO, 1822

Greg and Teri Heppe, Proprietors

In the early twentieth century, this general store consisted of a large two-story house, stable and shed, as well as a two-story store. The store was built by Deacon Leathers for the sum of $100 and has served the community since 1822. The Tuftonboro General Store offers everything from Band-Aids and groceries to pizzas and subs. The store still houses the Center Tuftonboro

Tuftonboro General Store, Middle Road (Route 109A), Center Tuftonboro, New Hampshire, circa 1822. "We want our visitors to feel as if they're in the nineteenth century when they come in." *Courtesy of author's collection.*

Post Office, which it has housed since 1851. The store has also been home for one of the town's libraries, a shoe shop and a stable.

A gentleman by the name of John A. Edgerly recalled that in the post–Civil War era, Tuftonboro Center, or Mackerel Corner as it was known in those days, was generally considered to be the seat of government for Tuftonboro. Here the people, mostly men, assembled and "wisely or unwisely, discussed the problems of the times."

The first storekeeper was Daniel Pickering, who sold it to Samuel Leavitt. Leavitt accumulated quite a fortune there and continued in business until his death. The property was then sold to Abel Haley and Andrew S. Hersey. At this time, Hersey made many improvements on the property. Many people came from different parts of the country to see this set of buildings, for there was not another set in the country to compete with them. In about two years, Haley and Hersey dissolved their partnership.

About the year 1860, Albert W. Wiggins went into partnership with Hersey. They remained together three or four years. During this time, there was a shoe shop in the second building where the shoes were made by hand.

During the 1870s, A.L. Hersey and A.W. Doe did an extensive poultry business. Mr. Hersey was postmaster for forty-eight years. It was common knowledge to many early residents that "Postmaster Herley was a very courteous gentleman and always had empty nail kegs and benches for the convenience of his customers. In cold weather, a large box stove, set in a frame filled with gravel or sawdust, was the target for the men who chewed tobacco. Many questions of state and national importance were discussed and settled here." Hersey had one son, Frank A. Hersey, who always remained with him so that when old age overtook Mr. Hersey, Frank was well fitted to take up the burden of the life that his father was about to lay down. Hersey died in 1895.

Frank began to do business in his own name and had a very good trade at the time. He carried a line of dry and fancy goods and also groceries. He was fortunate that the telephone and library were also here.

Over the years, there have been many owners of the old store, but since 1999, it has been owned and operated by Greg and Teri Heppe and Greg's son, Michael Wade. Today, it is considered a thriving and well-established landmark in the town. The Heppes have successfully managed to combine the past and present to keep the store alive as a living part of the community. To most people in town, it's just the local convenience store, meeting place and heart of Center Tuftonboro. It is the owners' mission to keep it as much as possible an old country store but still serve the community by providing updated goods and services.

"We want people to feel as if they're in the nineteenth century when they come in," Greg says, "yet it's not a museum or a tourist attraction. Its purpose is the same as when it was built in 1822—it's still a community store. Pantry staples, Band-Aids and convenience foods shore shelves with local products like Hunter's Bald Peak Farms maple syrup and Black Bear coffee."

The aroma of fresh-baked pizza pulls you back to the present. As I visited the store, many local citizens and visitors would come into the store to visit, have coffee, grab a can of soda and buy their lottery ticket on their way home from work.

Greg and Teri Heppe, retired schoolteachers from Wolfeborough, New Hampshire, thought they were downsizing when they came to Center Tuftonboro in 1999 to look at a modest cape. The real estate agent offered a walkthrough of another of her listings, the property across the street. The Heppes took one look and right away imagined themselves as storekeepers. They took a chance and bought the whole complex: a ten-room colonial, attached barn, two apartments and the store. They have been there ever since, managing the store and post office with some help from their grown children and grandchildren. The spacious table is the present site of many a meeting for the townspeople, and Michael's pizzeria supplies food for school, library and church events.

Interior with Mr. Heppe, proprietor, greeting his customers from his counter. *Courtesy of author's collection.*

The store advertises that it is "your one stop for dinner, propane, mail, gift items, movies, lottery tickets, coffee, ice and more."

The store is located on the Middle Road (Route 109A) in Center Tuftonboro, New Hampshire.

WEEKS & SMITH GENERAL STORE, MEREDITH, 1800s

Fred and Charles Weeks and Percy Smith, Proprietors

In 1838, Captain Joseph Lang started a dry goods business on Main Street at Post Office Square in what was originally known as the Lang Building. It later became a grocery store operated by John Knowles and then by Pease & Towle. Mr. Lang was better known as the captain of the Twelfth New Hampshire Volunteer Regiment during the Civil War. The hall above his store was used to recruit soldiers for the Twelfth Regiment.

Weeks & Smith General Store, Meredith Village, Meredith, New Hampshire. *From left to right*: Fred Weeks, Alpheus Hutchins, Charles Weeks, Percy Smith and Albert Kidder, circa 1800s. *Courtesy of the Meredith Historical Society.*

During the early 1900s, this building was the home of Weeks & Smith General Store.

In the mid-1900s, Sam Grad and sons Linden and Will also operated this property as a clothing store. Many businesses have come and gone since the Grads operated the store.

Today, the building is occupied by Bella-beads, Inspirational Touch, Dr. Hauschka—Facial Boutique, Kara's Café & Cakery, Mid-night Moon Tattoo and Refuge Salon.

The building is located at 48 Main Street across from the Meredith Historical Society in Meredith Village, New Hampshire.

ZEB'S GENERAL STORE, NORTH CONWAY, 1991

Peter Edwards and David Peterson, Proprietors

Zeb's General Store has achieved such a high level of recognition and popularity that it is considered one of the finest country stores in all of New England. The following history is found in its advertisement:

Opening for operations on July 7, 1991, with two hundred square feet of retail space, two employees and a dream to grow the largest emporium of New England made products, Zeb's General Store has achieved that goal with more than six thousand, six hundred square feet of retail space and thirty-six full and part-time employees. The largest collection of New England made specialty food in the world is found in the store's two-storied building accurately capturing the nostalgia of an "old time" mercantile. Zeb's provides an incubator of sorts for New England cottage-based businesses, as approximately eighty percent of sales come from the small businesses found in New Hampshire and surrounding New England states. Offering the chance to showcase new products to small cottage-based businesses is an important mission for the store and one that has not gone unnoticed.

Zeb's Store has earned many accolades and awards from Boston Magazine, the Retail Merchants Association of New Hampshire, and the Retailer of the Year by Pride of New England, as well as the Retailer of the Year by business New Hampshire Magazine.

Zeb's General Store is a virtual emporium of creativity from the largest collection of New England made specialty foods to soap, lotions, books, toys, pet items, artwork and photography and more. Try as you might, it would be very difficult to come away from Zeb's General Store without one or more items. From the old-fashioned Coca-Cola fountain to the claw foot bathtubs, penny candy counter and roughhewn wooden shelves, the mission to provide a nostalgic shopping experience is realized at every turn in the store.

Ask anyone in Mount Washington Valley, New Hampshire where to find the best shopping experience, and they'll point you to Zeb's General Store in the heart of North Conway Village. Reminiscent of its namesake, Zebulon Northrop Tilton, a colorful schooner captain, husband to three wives and New England folk hero, Zeb's General Store embodies the nostalgia of yesteryear with a decidedly whimsical flair.

Zeb's country store, Main Street, North Conway, New Hampshire. Zeb's General Store is an emporium of the largest collection of New England–made products for everyone, circa 1991. *Courtesy of David Peterson and Zeb's General Store.*

Inside the general store is seen the candy counter as it is today. The store is one of the most original stores in New Hampshire. It advertises, "If you can't find it just ask." *Courtesy of David Peterson and Zeb's General Store.*

Zeb's General Store is one of the most original stores of its kind in the state. The store is located on Main Street in North Conway, New Hampshire.

Chapter 6

Nostalgic Country Stores

REVIVE THE OLD COUNTRY STORE

On December 17, 2000, the *Boston Sunday Globe* staff writer Lois R. Shea recorded:

> *At the Harrisville Store, Dexter Gordon blows sweet and low on the tenor saxophone from the CD player; the tuna salad is made with herbs and lemon, the potato soup is fragrant with spice, and there's brie in the cheese case. But the basics are all here. Balsamic vinegar shares shelf space with Kraft macaroni and cheese. You can get batteries here, film, cough drops, Budweiser, videos and baby food—and organic yams, local eggs, fresh herbs, and cheddar cut right off the wheel.*

They are like our church steeples, farms and covered bridges. Without the precious landscape and rural setting, city folk would not come and visit us. The country landscape is distinct because it still has dirt roads, barns, clean forests, brooks, lakes and beautiful mountains to camp, hike and picnic in.

Many of our quiet little villages recline in valleys with blacksmith shops, schoolhouses, majestic white churches with their towering steeples, bed-and-breakfast homes and, of course, old country stores that reside prominently in the center of the village or square.

However, times are changing, and these fine little towns are struggling against the business tide. The old country store is a good example. The

Harrisville General Store as seen in Harrisville, New Hampshire, during the 1800s. *Courtesy of the Historic Harrisville Inc.*

Canterbury Country Store, a fixture in that town's history, closed its doors. The AG Burrows Store and the Red Brick Store, both from Sandwich, New Hampshire, are no longer in business. Boccia's in Claremont is gone, and if it weren't for some fine generous volunteer citizens, many more of the country stores and general stores would disappear with these. Some of these stores are now abandoned or have become museums. It appears that half of the country stores are barely surviving.

There are some concerned citizens in New Hampshire who realize, and others who are coming to understand, that general stores are more than just the sum of milk, bread and coffee. They are about community. The village store is a critical community service.

The modern convenience stores may be able to replace the milk and coffee part of what general stores traditionally provide, but they don't have porches. They don't have dusty wooden floorboards or a screen door that slams behind you just the way it slammed behind your grandfather. They don't have shopkeepers you recognize and who recognize you from behind the long wooden counter. Did you see the wooden Indian in the corner or on the front porch? How about the single gas pump in front of the porch or the old advertising signs and local town pictures on the wall inside the store?

The soup and beans are cheaper at the larger supermarkets, but are they worth it?

I, for one, would rather pay more for soup and have the opportunity to talk with my neighbors and friends and enjoy their fellowship than pay half the amount for my groceries and be completely impersonal.

Some of our village stores, such as the one in Freedom, New Hampshire, have formed a common cooperative to ensure historical preservation by buying the old defunct general stores and either renting them out or having volunteers run them.

Another good example is the Harrisville General Store building, which was bought by Historical Harrisville Inc. The organization has not only restored the build but has also revived the business. It has a general manager and board of directors that owns not only the store but also the mills across the canal.

Townspeople will tell you, "The place is full most every day. They come in to relax and talk. Now if they didn't do that they wouldn't see their neighbors from one end of the year to the other."

I understand that some people in Sandwich are exploring ways to save the old store, though I have heard that story before. In today's economy, small store owners face major hurdles. Wages for store workers have, in some cases, doubled in the past few years, and unlike the larger stores, they don't have the purchasing power to negotiate with suppliers.

LET'S GO SHOPPING—LET'S TRADE
Marion H. Robie

In 1970, Marion Horner Robie wrote a charming and interesting short story for the Tuftonboro Historical Society of her experiences. I would like to share a portion of this unpublished story with the reader:

> *A definition of the verb trade is "to barter; buy and sell." Very much of the acquiring of articles needed for the earliest farm homes, was done by barter, or exchange of products. Where there were no fixed prices, any agreement that seemed good to both parties could be quickly settled and the exchange of goods and services made while they were needed. The store, which would*

take anything that had any market value, expected to pay in other goods. A debtor could offer his labor, or that of his oxen, or build a chest, or raise a barn, or mow a field and such services seemed to be quite as good as cash.

Some of the earliest trade transactions are recorded in Marjorie Gene Harkness's book *The Fishbasket Papers* as follows:

January 30, 1809, Buy one Bushel and half potaters towards on lb. and ¼ of fethers that they had of us Since he had one lb. of fethers makes us even on that score by agreement.

September 9, 1812, I had one pair of mens shoes of Mr. Sanborn of Louden and let him have 2 sheep skins and I am to let him have 3 packs (pecks) of wheet or one Bushel of Ry and 4 lbs of good flacks for said Shose.

July 22, 1813, I had 11 lb of Rolls carded wanting 2 oz. and paid Daniel Hoit for carding the same. I let him have 7 lb. ¾ Butter which paid him fer carding and abought 3 quts Salt made us syhs on that accout. Also. Same date on 1813: I delievered Nathl Cram 27 lb. ¼ butter. 24 of which was for 2 Syhs that I had of him the first of this month. I had ¼ lb. tea for the remandir.

August 2ⁿᵈ, 3ʳᵈ, 4ᵗʰ 1813, Caleb Brown Dr. to my wife 3 day sewing for them with Suke Fowler for a Quarter of veal we had of him in July.

An account book of my great-grandfather, John Blazo, records charges and counter charges over a period of years. He used dollars and cents for value and had a set price for things exchanged. One account runs from April 13, 1827, to July 14, 1830, with a statement at the end: "This day settled all book accounts up to this date in full of all demands." It was signed John Blazo and Newbegin H. Mooney. Blazo had provided such items as:

2 maple logs 50 cents, one [man] had four oxen and wheels to Porter 2/3 of a day $1.75. Four gallons of applesauce at 25 cents per gallon $1.00. To wood, price agreed upon 20 cents. 7 ft of wood $1.09. 1/2 a bushel of corn, 4 cents. One day's work on the road 67 cents. 18 lb. Veal @ five cents per pound, 90 cents. Carrying grist mill and goin after it 34 cents.

Mr. Newbegin H. Mooney exchanged for the above such items as "horse nine miles to Eaton 36 cents. A sleigh, wood and paint $10.00. 9 lb. 1 oz. Mackeril $36.00 17 lb. 4 oz. Of salt fish, 3 1/2 cents per pound. One cheas [sic] press $2.50 and cash $2.88 to settle the account."

From some other early records, these items and their prices are interesting:

1. *Six dining chairs @ 8 shillings per chair $8.00.*
2. *One table pine leaf $2.00.*
3. *One rocking chair $3.50.*
4. *One pair thick leather shoes $1.50.*
5. *Forty-nine hemlock logs, 25 cents per log, $12.25.*
6. *Use of cider mill to make five barrels of cider 62 cents.*
7. *Weaving 11 3/4 yds of full cloth 86 cents.*
8. *Shearing five sheep 20 cents.*
9. *One pair of thick leather shoes. Price agreed upon three days work in haying.*
10. *One qt. Of W.I. Rum 25 cents.*
11. *One qt of N. rum 11 cents.*
12. *2 lb. 15 oz of pork for one meal of victuals and a hot dry baiting.*
13. *Running nine pewter spoons 9 cents.*
14. *Stick and timber for an axle tree 25 cents.*
15. *One gallon molasses 38 cents.*
16. *One string of bells $1.83.*
17. *8 lb. 7 oz of sapp shougar 10 cents lb. 85 cents.*
18. *One hand, one boy, a half a day binding shocks. 42 cents.*
19. *Four bushels of potatoes $1.00.*
20. *Hauling 29 bundles of hoops to Portland $ 7.00.*
21. *By reaping a piece of grain, price agreed on—two bushels of wheat.*
22. *One hat and a match safe, which I am to give two day's work for on the stable.*
23. *One logging and two meals for John 21 cents.*
24. *Twelve Punkings 4 cents a piece, 48 cents.*
25. *One bushel of black potatoes 50 cents.*
26. *Six hens, one of them a shanghai cock $2.25.*
27. *A pair of Giney hens 50 cents.*
28. *This day settled with J.A. Lowell and found due me one dollar, which I am to have in ashes.*
29. *30 quarts of milk on last years bill and 25 cent eggs $ 1.45.*

June 19, 1854 paid Simon Brown fifty cents for my part of painting the north end of the meeting house white.

April 28, 1857 Paid Charles Hurlin $2.00 for preachin.

Charles Hurlin Dr. to one half a cord of hard wood which he is to pay for the Free Will Baptist quarterly one year for $1.00.

A "Carroll County Pioneer" in 1857 advertised the following:

Steven Jackson, Window-Blind Manufacturer, at Moulton's Bedstead Factory, Ossipee Center, N.H. List of retail prices per window:

7 x 9, 12 lights 58 cents
8 x 10 "   "   65 cents
9 x 12 "   "   83 cents
7 x 9, 15 lights 65 cents
8 x 10 "   "   78 cents
9 x 13 "   "   98 cents

A diary kept by Marshall Piper, a local storekeeper in the Lakes Region, recorded the following:

I paid D.H. Durgin $12.25 for a coat and shirts, $3.45 for trimming and cutting of coat and a cap for $1.25.

In 1867, according to the cash accounts in back of his diary, he recorded:

I received $166.72 for a whole year and paid out $141.48, giving me a profit of $25.24. The following year I received a little more money, also spent more. I received $180.95 and spent $180.52, which left a gain of $.43 cents. This was the year I was married on December 24.

In 1871, Piper entered the following:

Jacob Hodgdon, Remick and I went to Meredith Village, got 92 bushels of corn. Paid $1.04 per bushel. Took dinner at Mr. Frank Kenney's. Went to Wolfeboro to get some boards for Ed Fernald's barn. Got 193 feet for 2 1/2 cents a foot, $4.82, plaining, 25 cents, Hauling boards $1.43, total $6.50.

In November, he worked for Wesley Canney for three and a half hours and half a day and received $1.87.

In Tuftonboro in 1867–71, Everett Doe's country store daybook gives some information on goods and prices paid during that period. This was soon after the Civil War when prices were considered high. I found one item dated March 3, 1868—just before Town Meeting Day.

Mr. Doe bought of H.N. Jordan & Company:

> *25 sheets sugar Bread 6 cents $1.50.*
> *25 sheets molasses Bread 5 cents $1.25.*
> *1 Box bread box   .15 cents*
> *1 Box oranges $4.75*

Mr. Doe's country store was stocked with groceries, hardware, dry goods, crockery, gunpowder, candy and the other typical items. Here are a few more examples of prices from his store: a barrel of flour sold for $10.00, molasses $0.65 per gallon, lard $0.21 per pound, sugar $0.15 per pound, two yards cambric for $0.24, one package undershirts $1.50, one axe handle $0.28, one straw hat $1.00, three bunches of matches $0.06, piece of beeswax $0.05, one bottle liniment $0.35, one parasol $0.50, one bag corn $2.10, four dozen crackers $0.24, harmonica $0.08, one package vases $0.25, round comb $0.30, one doll $0.25 and one bottle Opadildoc $0.25.

A 1962 *Granite State News* "Remember When" column, written by Bert Chamberlain of North Wolfeboro, gives some information about the practice of country stores buying pants made by local farmers' wives. The article specifically pertains to pants that were put together in Tuftonboro:

> *It seems odd to think that there was a period in our history when much of the store-bought clothing such as men's suits and pants were stitched together by farmers' wives and their daughters on the somewhat crude but dependable sewing machines of the time. In the back of her* [his mother's] *diary of 1880 she totaled her receipts for that year from three different agencies operating in the Parsonsfield area: "From Mr. Nute for making 185 coats, $58.45. From T Brackett & Son, 68 coats, $24.60. From Mr. Randall, 12 coats, $4.45." From 30 to 40 cts., according to size, was the pay for the labor of making a coat! I recall several women in the late 90s who still were doing sale work, but all complained of the small remuneration.*

The March 19, 1933 *Boston Sunday Globe* published an item about Melvin Village that is interesting. This was during the depression, the writer was John D. Pillsbury Jr. and the title of the article was "Back to Summer Haunt For a Winter Vacation." The following is an excerpt of the article:

It wasn't long before the reporter heard about the most startling news that had struck the village for a long time. Melvin Village had gone in for bartering!

During a fireplace conversation late that first night, George Howe told the reporter about the Melvin Village trading post. It was the first town in New Hampshire to adopt the system of swapping goods without the use of money. Here was something that was really news, and the reporter forgot that he was on a vacation the next morning when he set about to learn more about the trading post.

In Mrs. Amy Kling's modernized farmhouse and antique shop, the reporter sat down in a weather-beaten antique chair, which didn't squeak or wabble.

"It's too bad you won't be here next Monday," said Mrs. Kling. "Every Monday afternoon, between 2 and 4 o'clock, people from miles around gather in my barn. The eggs, potatoes, maple syrup, cream and all sorts of goods. And then the fun begins."

"One bright young woman," she said, "exchanged some silk underwear for a peck of potatoes, a quart of maple syrup, and a pound of beef."

A farmer with too much butter on hand gave a pound of butter for a bouquet of straw flowers to take home to his wife. Everybody reaches an agreement according to the age-old principle of supply and demand. Mrs. Kling showed him a copy of the Granite State News, Wolfeboro weekly, and pointed to the following notice: "Wanted—Two pigs and an electric washing machine in exchange for carpentry and electrical work. Apply Melvin Village Trading Post."

Mrs. Kling explained that the system started after Mrs. Elsie Howe let it be known that she had too much cream on hand and would exchange cream for potatoes. Mrs. Howe, Mrs. Kling and Mrs. Grace Severance were the women who started the ball rolling.

"Hardly anybody has much money, but there is only one family on the town welfare list, and they were helped along, even during the boom years," said Mrs. Horner.

Oscar Whedon, farmer, one of the best brook trout fishermen in the locality, took the reporter down into his cellar and showed him shelf after shelf loaded down with preserved vegetables and fruits that he had raised during the summer. Squash, spinach, cauliflower, all imaginable kinds of vegetables and fruit, were preserved in jars—at the last counting there were 508 jars on those shelves.

"That's the answer," said Mr. Whedon. "We only need enough money to buy such things as flour, sugar and coffee, and if we haven't enough for that, Mr. Horner gives us credit until business picks up in the summertime."

Nowadays every housewife talks about shopping for her groceries and other supplies. In the horse and buggy days, the word was trading. Often it meant literally just that, trading farm supplies—chiefly eggs and butter, sometimes salt pork and maple syrup—for groceries.

There is an old story about trading at the grocery store. A woman entered the store with a package of butter. She said quietly to the merchant, "I have some butter here that I would like to trade for some of yours. Frankly, a rat fell into the cream, so no one of my family will eat the butter. But I thought you could trade it as yours, and no one will ever know the difference. What they don't know won't hurt them."

The merchant took her butter and went to the rear room, but instead of exchanging it for some of his own, he rewrapped hers, returned it to the woman and told her, "What people don't know won't hurt them any."

Marion Robie reflects on some early years with the country store in her story:

You might be interested to know that when my father first stocked his store in 1894, he went by horse drawn team with Herbert Hodgdon of Tuftonboro Corner to Portland, Maine where Herb introduced him to the wholesalers with whom he was doing business.

My early memory of our store is of long hours of being open, especially in the summer when there was a boat operating between Melvin Village and The Weirs and Lakeport that carried mail. It left Melvin about 6 o'clock in the morning and that meant getting the mailbags ready to leave the Post Office before the hour of the boat's departure. Breakfast was eaten after that, but there were frequent interruptions by customers who had no qualms about coming to the back door and asking for groceries and a plug of tobacco. In most instances things were charged.

Our store was a place for social gatherings in the evenings. Many wonderful yarns have been spun there. In the winter, a checkerboard was provided for entertainment and skill. The store would remain open until 9 o'clock in the evening or even later.

When I first took over the bookkeeping for my father, I was considered insolent when I endeavored to educate our customers to honor the innovation of receiving and paying the bills that I sent out each month. I remember one account that had been running for years, with many debits and credits of eggs and salt pork, with an occasional hen for our own use. Naturally, it was a bird that was not a layer. This customer of a seeming never ending settlement was very disturbed. Hadn't something been given on account at intervals? Yes, except in the summer when they sold their eggs and chickens to the summer people. It took a lot of time and persuasion to finally get them to try to make a settlement each month.

Last year the Granite State News published a list of 18 different items of food, such as butter, cream, eggs, fish, 7 kinds of meat, cheese, flour, sugar and potatoes with their prices. In 1932, the peak year of the recession, the total list could be bought for $3.75. In 1940 the food items totaled $5.15, and in 1969 the same list of groceries cost $14.83. According to the Bureau of Employment Security in Concord, the average weekly wage in this area in 1940 was $21.48, whereas the average weekly wage in 1969 was $115.00.

Marion Horner Robie
May 24, 1970

THE TRADITIONAL CIGAR STORE INDIAN

Several years ago, an article appeared in a local newspaper in Tuftonboro, New Hampshire, about a life-sized wooden Indian to be placed in the Tuftonboro Country Store, which was to symbolize the tradition of the cigar store Indian. The story was written by staff writer Sarah Schell for the *Granite State News*. An excerpt of the article follows:

Tuftonboro—Frequent visitors to the Tuftonboro General Store have undoubtedly seen the authentic style Cigar Store Indian that has made its home in the corner of the main room of the store properly stationed next to the wood stove. On Thursday, July 1, 2004, Tuftonboro artist Brian Stockman delivered this very impressive, seven-foot tall sculpture made of white pine to the store. The lifelike, full-size wooden Indian makes a powerful impression. Bright colors and earth tones accent the chief's expressive face and strong body.

Brian began with a 24-inch wide log, and with a chainsaw followed by hand gauges of various sizes to create his sculpture.

The traditional cigar store Indian welcomes you to Tuftonboro's general store. Located inside the store, near the fireplace, is a magnificent wooden carving of a life-sized Indian. On July 1, 2004, Tuftonboro artist Brian Stockman delivered this most impressive seven-foot-tall sculpture made of white pine to the store. *Courtesy of author's collection.*

Brian Stockman is a native to Tuftonboro and grew-up with a very creative family. His father Philip Stockman, owner of Country Furniture in Center Tuftonboro, had a strong influence on his son's artistic ability.

Storeowner Greg and Teri Heppe are thrilled about acquiring this new addition to the old-fashioned Country Store. The Indian joins other old features such as a woodstove, a cheese case, and a coffee mill. When Greg Heppe bought the old historic store, it was his desire to restore it to its original appearance—which he has done!

Greg Heppe said about Brian Stockman that, "one of the things that makes this special is that he knows what 18ᵗʰ century Indians actually looked like." Greg Heppe talked with Brian about the possibility of making the Indian specifically for the store.

"It's been in the works for a couple of years," said Brian. "I really got cranking on it just after Christmas and finished it a few weeks ago."

The Heppes are seriously considering calling the statue "Chief Paugus" after a 1720s Ossipee Indian chief name Paugus.

Brian Stockman proudly watches it all from beside the plate of glass windows decorated with snowmen, and a hand painted sign points the way to the post office in the back of the store.

THE WEATHERMEN

City men seldom think about the weather, while country folk seldom forget it. Weather was an intimate reality to the farmer, who watched carefully the phases of the moon, the slow turning of the seasons and any striking portent in the evening sky. Each out-of-the-ordinary occurrence was likely to be set down in the country merchant's chronicle, similar to one country store's account book with a note on a year of drought: "The hay crop in the summer of 1862 was about half a crop." A man could learn a lot about weather signs around a country store if he was of a mind to listen. The following excerpts contain advice of the time recorded by historian Gerald Carson in *The Old Country Store*:

Frost come six weeks after you hear the first katydid.

Plant root crops in the dark of the moon; if you don't they will go all to tops.

When you blow out a candle, if the wick smolders a long time, bad weather is in prospect. If it goes out quickly the weather will be fair.

When the camphor bottle is "riley" a storm is brewing.

Frost is out of the ground when you hear the first frogs.

Plant corn when the oak leaves are the size of a squirrel's ear.

Tomato plants set out when the sign is in the Twins, will bear smooth tomatoes.

The countryman needed the most reliable information he could get about rain. "Rain before seven," they said, "Clear before 'leven." When chimney smoke falls to the ground that means rain. Sundogs predict rain. A ring around the moon means stormy weather. Rub a cat's fur the wrong way, and sparks will mean cold weather. The last Friday in each month sets the weather for the next month. Other signs of rain were frisky animals, the cry of tree toads, a mackerel sky, mare's tails streaked across the sky. A buzzing in telegraph wires meant a change in the weather.

A hard winter was coming when the squirrels put away a big store of nuts. This evidence could be validated by examining the husks on the corn. If they were thicker than usual and the apple skins were tougher, the squirrels were right! Not precisely weather data, but a useful saying around a farm was the rhyme:

On Candlemas Day
Half the wood
And half the hay.

My father-in-law always looked to the mountains from his home in North Sandwich to predict the weather: "When the first snow appeared on the summit of Mount Chocorua; we could expect a snowstorm within two weeks."

THE TRUE YANKEE

What is the point of talking if you don't have something important to say?

The true Yankee resents unnecessary words. He also fails to be enthusiastic about advice offered to him. Thus it was with Neighbor Sam Perkins, who, with his employer, went out one day to grind some wheat. As the work started, Sam sat down on the overturned box to grind. This aroused in his employer an expression of contempt, the bulk of his remarks being that Sam would never get rich by sitting down on the job. Sam's retort, which closed the debate, was this: "I've known men to get rich by minding their own business."

This finality of reply is one of the most typical characteristics of the old-fashioned Yankee that I am sure you would meet in the old country store. We have not yet improved on it. How it developed in the conversations by the store would be difficult to say. Certainly the early settlers did not bring it from England. It is serviceable in our country life and is equally useful applied in a wider field. Most of us instinctively like to argue. Our replies are likely to be made for the purpose of provoking one another. The real natives of New Hampshire did just the opposite. Their purpose was to say something that would stop the talk.

This account is found in the simple affairs of village trading and personal business, thus the difference of opinion between two brothers who live in a town just south of the Lakes Region.

These two did not get along well together. Finally their affairs came to a crisis, and one of them left the homestead and moved to Meredith Bridge. He took the horse with him.

The brother who remained thought the situation over and then followed the other to the bridge. He approached his brother and presented this brief but comprehensive summing up of the situation and outline of his purpose: "I've come for the horse, and I shall take it home. I shall take the head part, and if you want your part, you can cut it off"—to which there was no adequate reply.

TOWN MEETING

There was, however, plenty of talk at the annual town meeting, which might explain the close association between our early government and membership in the Protestant church of the time. If, in the town meeting, the minister did the talking, the individual citizen had his say. This town custom developed as intended with a high degree of intelligent interest on the part of the people in all town affairs. They came to the meeting well informed and eager to express their opinion. Sometimes the moderator was a dictator who succeeded in restricting free speech, but usually the contrary was the case.

The town meeting was a great place for talk, but it was not the only place; there was the village store on the first floor of the building—that was the center of perpetual political conversation. People met there by custom as stated earlier. For refreshments they had dried apples, prunes, crackers and salt codfish. (In those days, salt codfish did not come packed in wooden boxes. The fish, dried and salted in its original shape, hung from the ceiling. It was not nearly as clean and free from bones as seen in our markets today, but it had a salty tang to it that has been lost in these more hygienic days.)

There, amid the hardware—accompanied by chewing tobacco, pipes and, on cold days, an iron stove in the center of the room—the affairs of state and nation were discussed. If the New Hampshire town meeting suggested the framework on which our national government scheme was built, it was equally true that the American political convention began in the country general store.

It is a fair conclusion that our natives from New Hampshire, in the days when their characteristics were most pronounced, were not uncommunicative so much as discriminating. They had no halting utterance when it appeared to them that they might speak to a purpose.

The cartoon speaks for itself: a town meeting. *Courtesy of Tuftonboro General Store.*

For example, when I anxiously asked the storekeeper if he knew where the men's room was, he replied with equal force, "Ayah!" and promptly strolled away. Country folk had a dislike for wasting words.

Let us now return to the second floor of the country store, where the town meeting was in progress, and yet another example of this type of country humor.

At the Old Country Store in Moultonborough, for example, early town meetings were held in the second-floor assembly room on the second Tuesday in March of each year. In these meetings, silence did not always reign.

The fundamental theory of the town meeting was that the local citizens should, and did, have a right to express freely their views for or against any and every proposed article relating to town affairs. Sometimes in these meetings in the country store's assembly room, one man's voice was as loud as another's. The town meeting was based on thought, words and action. It is our greatest heritage.

The rhetoric displayed at some of the town meetings has been well recorded with the knowledge that it should surely be remembered, especially when Percy Doolittle was in attendance; he was the hermit near the Lower

Falls. These meetings were not complete without some resolution or motion being proposed by old Percy, and this particular year (1863) was no exception. As the moderator proceeded to close the meeting, old Percy piped up:

Mistur Moderator! In respect to the protection of Henroosts, I've got here in my seat and heared the opponents of this great measure expectorate again it 'til I am purty nigh busted with indignant commotions of my lacerated.

Mistur Moderator! Are it possible that men can be so infaturated as to vote against this motion?

Mistur Moderator! Allow me to picture to your excited and denuded imagination some of the heart rendering evils which arise from the want of purtection to he-roosts in my vicinity.

Mistur Moderator! We will suppose it to be the awful and melancholy hour of midnight. All nature em hushed in deep repose. The solumn wind softly moans through the wavin' branches of the trees and nought is heard to break the solemncholy stillness, save the occasional grunt from the hog pen. I will now carry you in imagination to that devoted hen house. Behold its peaceful and happy inmates greatly inclining in balmy slumber on their elevated and majestic roosts. Look at the aged, venerable, and highly respected rooster, as he keeps his silent vigils with patience and unmitigated watchfulness over those innocent, helpless and virtuous pullets. Just let your eyes glance around that dignified and matronly and peternal con gradulations over those little juvenile chickens, who crowd around their respective progenitor and nestle under his circumbiant wings.

Now I ask you, Mistur Moderator, am there to be found a wretch so lost and abandoned as will enter that peaceful and happy abode and tear those interestin' little bibbies from their aronized and hear-broken parents?

Mistur Moderator! I answer in huntder tones, there am. Are there anythin' so mean and sneakin' as such a robbery? No! there are not! You may search the wide universe from the natives who repose in solitary grandeur and superlative majesty under the shade of the tall cedar that grow upon the tops of the Himmalah Mountains in the Valley of Jehasephet, down to the degraded and barbarous savages who repose in the obscurity in their miserable wigwams in the Rock of Gilbralter, in the Gulf of Mexico, and then you will be so much puzzled to find anythin' so mean, as you would to see the rath revolved around the sun once in twenty-four hours without the aid of a telescope.

Mistur Moderator! I feel that I have said enough on the subject to convince the most obstinate member of the unapproachable necessary of a law which shall forever and everlastingly put a stop to these fowl proceedings, and I propose that every convicted offender shall suffer the penalty of the law as follows:

Mistur Moderator! All I want is for every member of this house to act on this subject accordin' to his conscientiousness. Let him do this and he will be remembered everlastingly by a grateful posterity.

Mistur Moderator! I've done! Where's my hat?

The eloquent gentleman donned his sealskin cap and sat down, apparently much exhausted. It is not, however, the purpose of this section to enter on a discussion of the principles and ideals of our early government and its town meeting, nor debate its methods, except to show that we find manifested today from our heritage of our New Hampshire town meetings that we will speak freely and to the point.

COUNTRY STORE HUMOR
Storytellin' and Small Talk

When there was no stove in the store, the rural philosophers would gather around the fireplace. Sometimes the sitters seemed to be just a social club, a forum for democratic debate, but the store also provided a receptive audience for the telling of tall tales.

The topics discussed ranged over many fields of interest and gossip—the new preacher, who was the state of grace and the idea of Immaculate Conception, as well as some modern instances of the ordinary kind. They talked of birth and death, of government and elections and always of the weather. Here the old soldier shouldered his crutch and showed how fields were won. And here the story of the awkward swain was passed around, how he took his girl to the county fair in a buggy. As they drove past the popcorn stand, the young lady remarked, "My, that popcorn smells good." And his reply, "Tell you what, I'll drive up close's I can so you can smell it real good."

It's not all buying, selling or trading at the old store—there is socializing and town meetings. As I said earlier, there is a certain breed of people that frequents the country store. Many of the customers enjoy just sitting around near the stove and reminiscing and telling stories, political and otherwise. If you listen very closely, you can tell whether these people are locals or tourists.

The front porch local contentedly watches patiently as the city flatlander fills his car with gas. *Courtesy of Roselyn Grossholz.*

The real New Hampshire native has a reputation for extreme silence, except when absolutely necessary. This manner of speaking presents a paradox: he is at once the most silent and the most talkative of men.

Let me cite some examples of the type of country humor.

On one occasion, a summer resident who, while driving home, came upon a farmer's boy whose hay load toppled over and lay in a great heap by the side of the road. The boy was engaged in pulling the hay to one side. The city man, after a very brief but not very productive conversation, persuaded the boy to come home with him and have some lunch.

"You come and rest and eat, and then after lunch, I'll get some of my men to help you get your hay back on the wagon."

Reluctantly, the boy accompanied the other toward the nearby house, but as he went he kept muttering to himself: "Father won't like it."

Finally, the older gentleman stopped in disgust and faced the youth.

"What is your problem?" he questioned. "Why won't your father like it?"

"Because," replied the boy, "he is under the hay load."

A Little Bit Deaf in Her Years

There is a story of a deaf old lady who walked in the village store and asked for five cents' worth of castile soap.

"We don't sell a nickel's worth," replied the clerk politely.

"Yes, I want the white kind," she answered pleasantly.

"You don't understand me, madam: I said a nickel wouldn't buy any castile soap in this establishment."

"Sure enough," replied the aged customer, "soap isn't what it used to be in my time; they put too much rozum in it nowadays."

"Oh, Lord!" said the now distracted clerk in a stage whisper, "will you listen to this old lunatic?" Placing his mouth to the dame's ear, he fairly screamed, "We don't sell a nickel's worth of soap here!"

"Yes," smiled the old lady, "I wish you would wrap it up securely with a double thickness of paper; I don't want it smelling up my bag."

The clerk rushed to a box, took out a bar of soap, and almost threw it at the old woman, exclaiming, "Take it and get out, you old harridan of thunderation!"

She smiled, wrapped it herself and carefully laid her nickel on the counter. "You're the politest and most accommodating young man I ever seen, and I'll call again when I need more soap."

Taking Castor Oil

A young lady came into the general store and asked the storekeeper if it was possible to disguise castor oil. "It's horrid stuff to take, you know. Ugh!"

"Why certainly," said the storekeeper. Another young lady sat down at the back counter and ordered a chocolate ice cream soda. The storekeeper asked the first customer if she would not have one too. With a smile she accepted the invitation and drank it down with much gusto.

"Now tell me, sir, how would you disguise castor oil?"

He beamed all over. "Aha, my dear young lady, I just gave you some—in that soda—"

"But, good heavens, Sir! Why, I wanted it for my sister!"

Making Conversation

There is a quiet little town in New Hampshire—that is, they call it a town; you blink and you've missed it. Back in the hills are the logging camps, a small shack, a nearby railroad stop. There is one building in the village—a combined general store and lunchroom, which for six days a week is no more crowded than a Methodist revival meeting in a Jewish neighborhood.

A stranger, hiking through the hills near Whiteface Mountain, came to this general store and decided to have some lunch. After the waitress had served him, she regarded him favorably from the door, wondering how she could start a conversation, for it was a lonely place.

At last she spoke, looking through the door. "It looks like rain," she volunteered.

He sniffed once at the steaming cup. "Yes," he said, "it does, but it smells like coffee."

Wasn't He Right?

A shrewd old country farmer from the east side of Big Lake went into a general store near Wolfeborough and asked the price of bread.

"Eight cents a loaf."

"Ah," said the farmer briskly. "I'll just take a loaf." The clerk rolled it up for him. As he took the parcel, a new thought struck him.

"How much are those cans of tomatoes?"

"Eight cents," said the startled the clerk.

"Oh, ah," said the customer thoughtfully; then, with great rapidity, "Well, I won't take the bread, I'll take the tomatoes; bread's eight cents; tomatoes are eight cents; give me the tomatoes—here's the bread," and he passed over the loaf, took the tomatoes, stuck them into his pocket and started out.

"See here," interrupted the clerk, "you haven't paid for the tomatoes."

"Paid for it? Of course I haven't! I gave you the bread for it, both the same price, you know."

"Yes, I know," said the clerk, who was getting confused, "but you didn't pay for the bread."

"Pay for it!" thundered the farmer. "Of course I didn't! Why should I? I'm not takin' it am I?"

And then the clerk said meekly, "Oh, well, I presume it's all right—only I don't. But of course you're correct—only, if you'd just as soon leave, I wish you'd trade somewhere else." After half an hour's study of the problem, the clerk said sadly, "Well, anyway, he was a darn smart man."

The Obliging Creditor

The village people were out collecting subscriptions for a new Methodist church. One of the collectors met Uncle Percy in front of his country store and asked him how much he was going to give.

"Can't give a cent."

"Why you must contribute something!"

"No, sir; I owe too much money—I must be just before I'm generous."

"Yes, but you owe God a larger debt than you do anyone else."

"That may be so, but He ain't a-pushin' me like my other creditors."

Ascending Straight to Heaven

"You must tiptoe upstairs, and take a look at little Mary before she is asleep," said the proud mother.

The visitor followed her up to the nursery. The two grown people looked in; there was the little girl, on her knees beside the big bed.

"Isn't that a picture!" whispered the mother fondly, "Innocence, saying her prayers to the Heavenly Father!"

Just then the little girl's voice floated out to them. "Where in de debbil did I leave dat dolly?"

Sympathy Spurned

The elderly spinster sniffed when anyone suggested that it was too bad she did not have a husband.

"I have a dog that growls, a parrot that swears, a fireplace that smokes and a cat that stays out all night. Why should I want a husband?"

The Question

In the country store's small luncheon area, a guest called out sharply, "Storekeeper!"

"Yes sir."

"What's this?"

"It's your soup, sir."

"Yes, but what kind of soup?"

"It's bean soup," said the storekeeper with dignity.

"I'm not asking what it's been; I'm asking what it is now!"

Pharmaceutical

"I want some consecrated lye," said the customer to the storekeeper.

"You mean concentrated lye."

"It does nutmeg any difference," the man retorted. "That's what I camphor. How much does it sulphur?"

"Fifteen scents. Bright fellow, aren't you? I never cinnamon with so much wit."

"Well, I should myrrh-myrrh! And as yet ammonia beginner at it."

Error

One of the guests turned to a man by his side to criticize the singing of the woman who was trying to entertain them.

"What a terrible voice! Do you known who she is?"

"Yes," was the answer, "She's my wife."

"Oh, I beg your pardon. Of course, it isn't her voice, really. It's the stuff she has to sing. I wonder who wrote that awful song?"

"I did," was the answer.

CLOSING REMARKS ON NEW HAMPSHIRE'S COUNTRY STORE

Gerald Carson's *The Old Country Store* describes the New Hampshire country store quite well:

> We have an impression of the droll stories told around the general store by a man with an original vein in him. We should not suppose that his perceptions were insensitive as he listened to the secret sound of snow water, trickling water under ice at sugaring-off time. For men do not speak of such matters. A man could not in all decency say that he had lifted up his eyes unto the hills, unless he made it clear and plain that he was simply quoting from the Bible. He could not tell of a time when his heart leaped as he watched his mare and her colt at play in the upper meadow; but it was entirely fit and proper to discuss an interesting case of heartburn. And if he did, a good deal of lore about medicine and health would be made available to him at once, some having to do with the patents, the proprietary which stood in rows on the store shelves, some having to do with

The Shannon Store daybook sample of accounts. *Courtesy of Steve Holden.*

old medications made up from traditional family recipes and compounded in the home kitchen. None were without effect if they contained enough alcohol.

These narratives have dwelt on traditional sayings, bodacious tales, jokes and capers because the evidence is so abundant that the old country store provided the perfect environment for the cultivation of these lively arts. To deal adequately with rural New Hampshire, as the early visitors did, it should be recognized that there was another side to the life of the local people in the Granite State who lived on the bosom of nature. They had a vein of sentiment and a caring attitude for their neighbors.

Some morning before nine o'clock, make a visit to the general store in Tuftonboro, and you might enjoy the truth in my stories of the old country store.

Bibliography

Bacon, George F. *The Country Store*. Boston, MA: Mercantile Publishing Company, 1890.

Carson, Gerald. *The Old Country Store*. New York: E.P. Dutton & Company, 1965.

Cushing, Kenneth E. *Isinglass, Timber, and Wool: A History of the Town of Grafton, NH, 1761–1992*. Grafton, NH: privately printed, 1992.

Gould, R.E. *Yankee Storekeeper*. New York: Whittlesey House, 1946.

Grossholz, Roselyn. *Country Store Collectables Price Guide*. Des Moines, IA: Wallace-Homestead Book Company, 1972.

Harrison, Jim. *Country Stores*. Atlanta, GA: Longstreet Press, 1993.

Holden, Steve. *The Old Country Store*. Moultonborough, NH: Harvest Press, 1991.

Kalman, Bobbie. *Early Stores and Markets*. New York: Crabtree Publishing Company, 1981.

Musgrove, Richard W. *History of the Town of Bristol: Grafton County, New Hampshire*. 2 vols. Bristol, NH: R.W. Musgrove, 1923.

Sandwich Historical Society and Jane Beckman. *Sandwich, New Hampshire 1763–1990*. Edited by Patricia Heard and Shirley Elder Lyons. Portsmouth, NH: Peter E. Randell, 1990.

Smith, Elmer L. *Country Store: The General Store of Yesterday*. Lebanon, PA: Applied Arts Publishers, 1977.

Squires, James D. *The New Hampshire General Store, New Hampshire*. Vol. 2. N.p.: American Historical Company, 1956.

Ward, Barbara M., ed. *Produce and Conserve, Share and Play Square: The Grocer and the Consumer on the Home Front Battlefield during World War II*. Portsmouth, NH: Strawbery Banke Museum, 1994.

Youth's Companion 66, no. 13 (1893) "The Old Leather Man.".

Index

Index

T

Taylor & Bond 91
telephone 16, 20, 93
Tilton 63, 83
tobacco 9, 16, 23, 31, 45, 59, 74, 78, 93, 112
tonic 27, 28
town meeting 16, 79, 105, 112, 115
trade 5, 13, 19, 21, 35, 37, 39, 41, 58, 63, 72, 73, 78, 88, 93, 101, 107, 118
Tuftonboro 7, 23, 80, 91, 94, 105, 107, 108, 122

W

weathermen 110
Weeks & Smith 94
wooden Indian 23, 24, 27, 34, 41, 82, 108, 109

Y

Yankee 5, 35, 42, 111, 123

Z

Zeb's 7, 96

About the Author

Dr. Bruce D. Heald, PhD, is a graduate of Boston University, the University of Massachusetts–Lowell and Columbia Pacific University. He is an adjunct associate professor at Babes-Bolyai University in Cluj, Romania, and presently an adjunct professor of American history at Plymouth State University, Plymouth, New Hampshire. Dr. Heald is presently a fellow in the International Biographical Association and the World Literary Academy in Cambridge, England. Dr. Heald is a recipient of the Gold Medal of Honor for literary achievement from the American Biographical Institute (1993). From 2005 to 2008, he was a state representative to the General Court of New Hampshire. He resides in Meredith, New Hampshire, with his family.